The

Garden Diary
Journal
&
Log Book

by

Joy L. Kieffer

The Garden Diary, Journal & Log Book: Plan garden beds and track changes in your landscape for a year to year record. 100 diary pages, 10 graph pages and 10 lined pages opposite for notations. Pest and disease prevention, plant propagation, zone map, weights, measures and conversion tables included.
For those who want a simpler format or need additional diary and plotting graphs for additional beds. All pages are taken directly from The Garden Journal, Planner & Log Book.

Published by Hidden Cache Media
Copyright 2016 Joy L. Kieffer, Wallingford, PA
Artwork and cover design by Joy L. Kieffer
Author photos by HR Kelley

ISBN-13: 978-0-9981078-0-6
ISBN-10: 0-9981078-0-8

Available from Amazon.com, and other retail outlets.
Available in bulk quantities. Visit www.gardenkitch.com to see the original and more comprehensive The Garden Journal, Planner & Log Book, other available formats, other books in the series or other garden-related items. Email contact@gardenkitch.com for bulk orders for garden clubs, fundraisers or reseller pricing.

~ Dedication ~

To all the intrepid gardeners out there who continue to be optimistic in the face of weather, pestilence and self-sabotage.

~ Acknowledgements ~

None of this would be possible without the One who designed and created the first garden with its unlimited potential, and then turned it over to us in the greatest display of faith imaginable.

I want to thank my husband and daughters, interns and volunteers ~ who have tolerated and in some cases abetted my delusions of grandeur as I dream of perfection in our various gardens.

And last, I want to thank all the various supporters of the Lifewerks Giving Garden. A portion of the proceeds of the books from the Garden Journal Log Book series will go to support the Lifewerks Giving Garden and Lifewerks mentoring programs.

~ ABOUT THIS BOOK ~

These diary pages and the combined graph and lined pages for garden plots are taken directly from *The Garden Journal, Planner & Log Book*. This book is for those who want just these three simple forms to write down and draw out the information about their garden spaces in a separate book, or have run out of room in the larger, and more comprehensive Garden Journal.

Several of the forms from *The Garden Journal, Planner & Log Book* are available in booklet form singly or combined for those of you who want more room than that journal provides. Look for these on Amazon or at gardenkitch.com.

A note: This is your book. Use it or abuse it as your needs dictate. Cover it with waterproof film, take it to your local printer and have the spine cut off and the pages hole-punched or put into a spiral binding. Just don't copy the book — that's all I ask. I wouldn't give away your services for free, so I hope you will understand that I want to make a profit for my family's needs and to support great causes like the Lifewerks Giving Garden.

For the comprehensive garden journal with 28 different forms, please check out The Garden Journal, Planner & Log Book. Put it on your Amazon Wish List and recommend it to your friends. By doing so, you will encourage better ratings, and therefore, more donations to our great cause. The Lifewerks Giving Garden food pantry and garden and the Lifewerks mentoring programs. (See lifewerks.org for more info.)

Thank you ~

Joy

P.S. ~ It would be terrific if you would leave a review on Amazon if you find that you like your Garden Diary and Planner, and it would be great if you buy more for friends!

U. S. Plant Zone Map

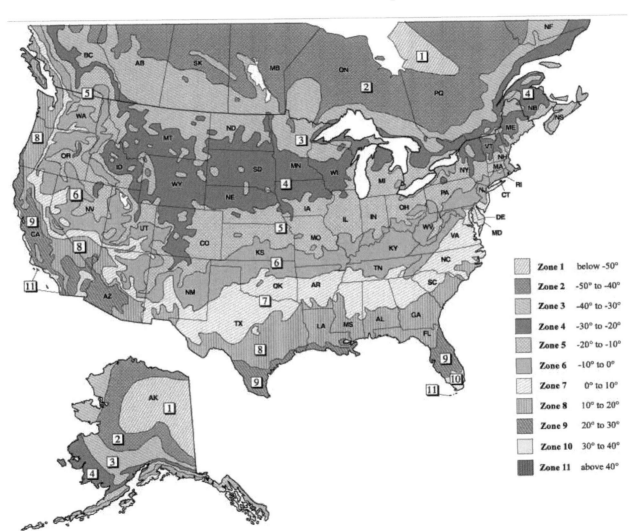

	Zone 1	below -50°
	Zone 2	-50° to -40°
	Zone 3	-40° to -30°
	Zone 4	-30° to -20°
	Zone 5	-20° to -10°
	Zone 6	-10° to 0°
	Zone 7	0° to 10°
	Zone 8	10° to 20°
	Zone 9	20° to 30°
	Zone 10	30° to 40°
	Zone 11	above 40°

Garden Plot:

Garden Plot: _____

_____

_____

_____

_____

_____

_____

_____

_____

_____

_____

_____

_____

_____

_____

_____

_____

_____

_____

_____

_____

_____

_____

_____

Garden Plot:

Garden Plot:

Garden Plot: _____

Garden Plot: _____

_____

_____

_____

_____

_____

_____

_____

_____

_____

_____

_____

_____

_____

_____

_____

_____

_____

_____

_____

_____

Garden Plot: _____

_____

_____

_____

_____

_____

_____

_____

_____

_____

_____

_____

_____

_____

_____

_____

_____

_____

_____

_____

_____

_____

_____

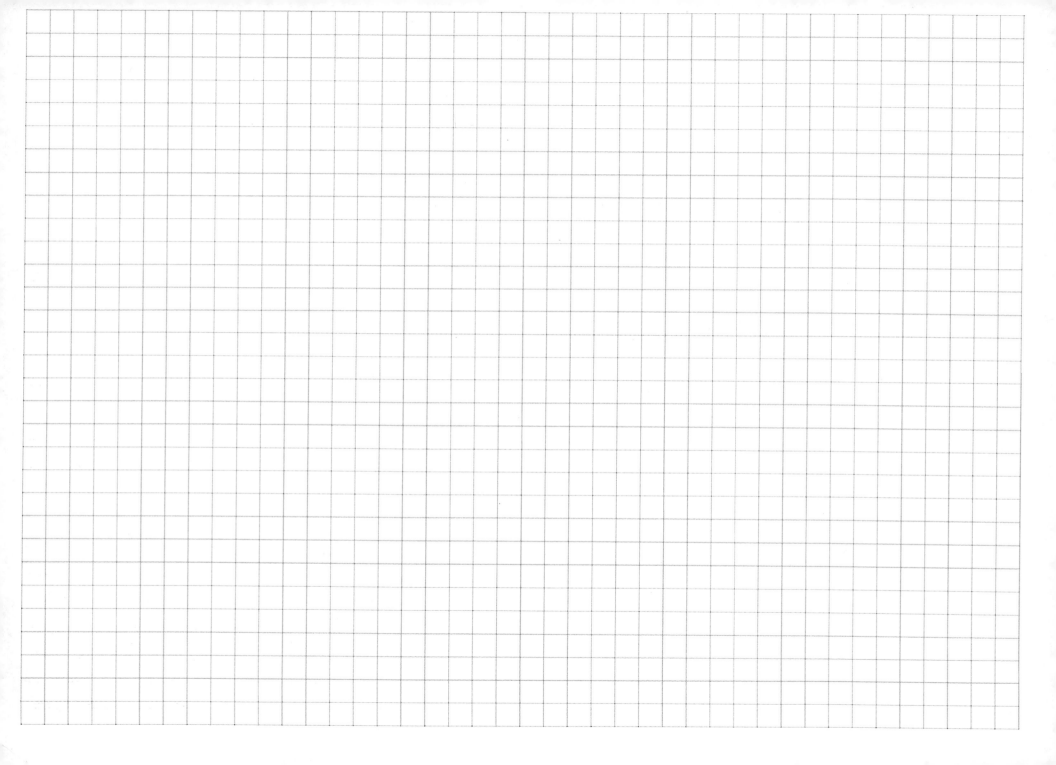

Garden Plot:

Garden Plot:

Garden Plot:

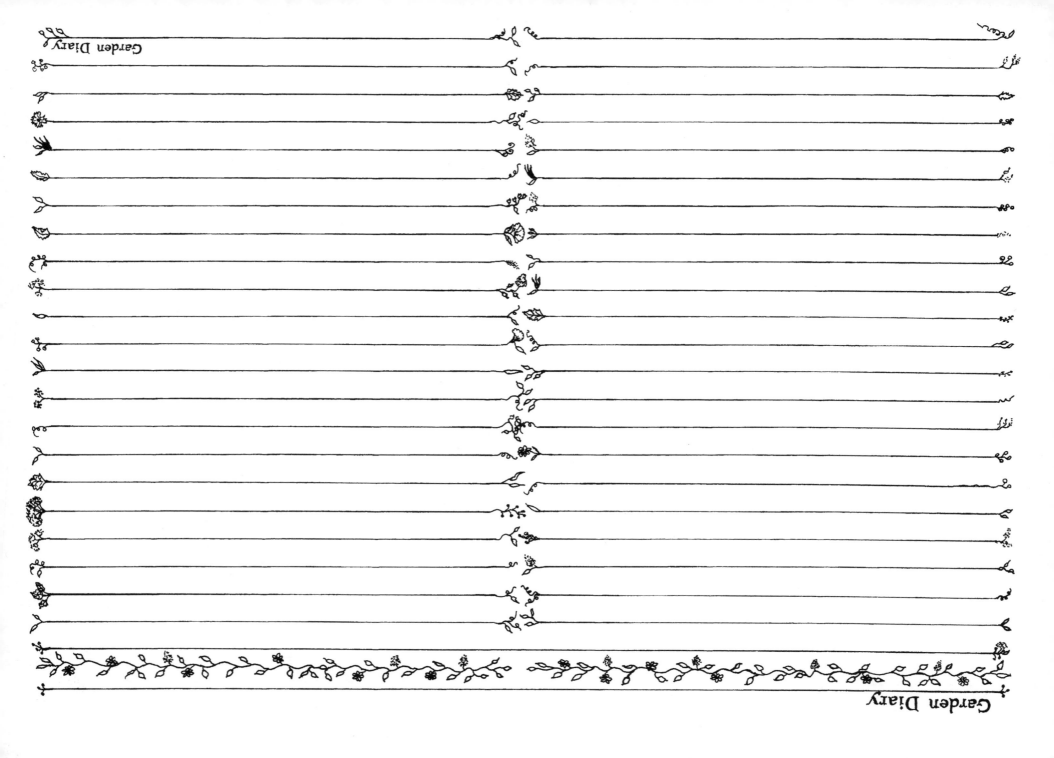

Garden Diary

Garden Diary

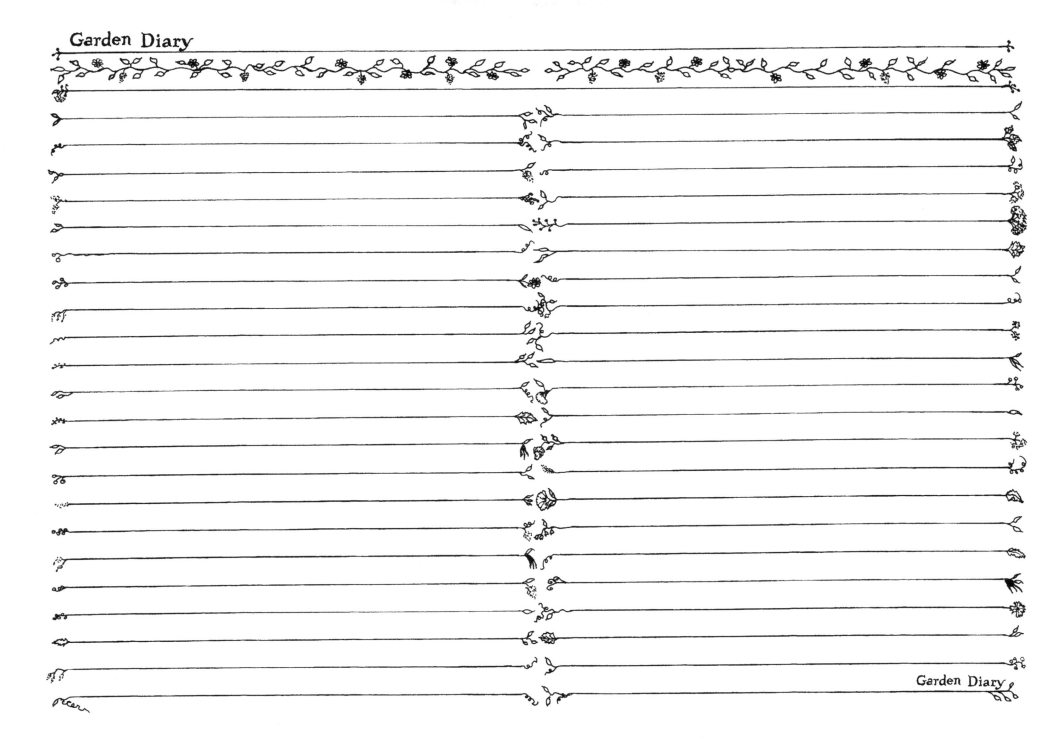

Garden Diary

Garden Diary

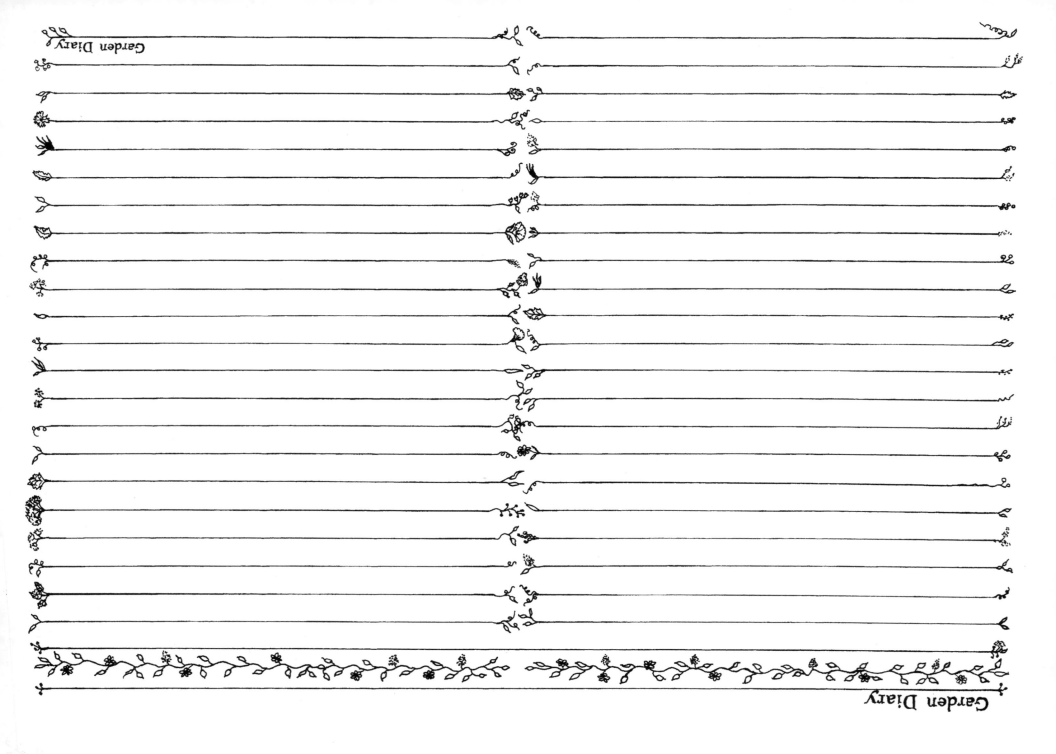

Garden Diary

Garden Diary

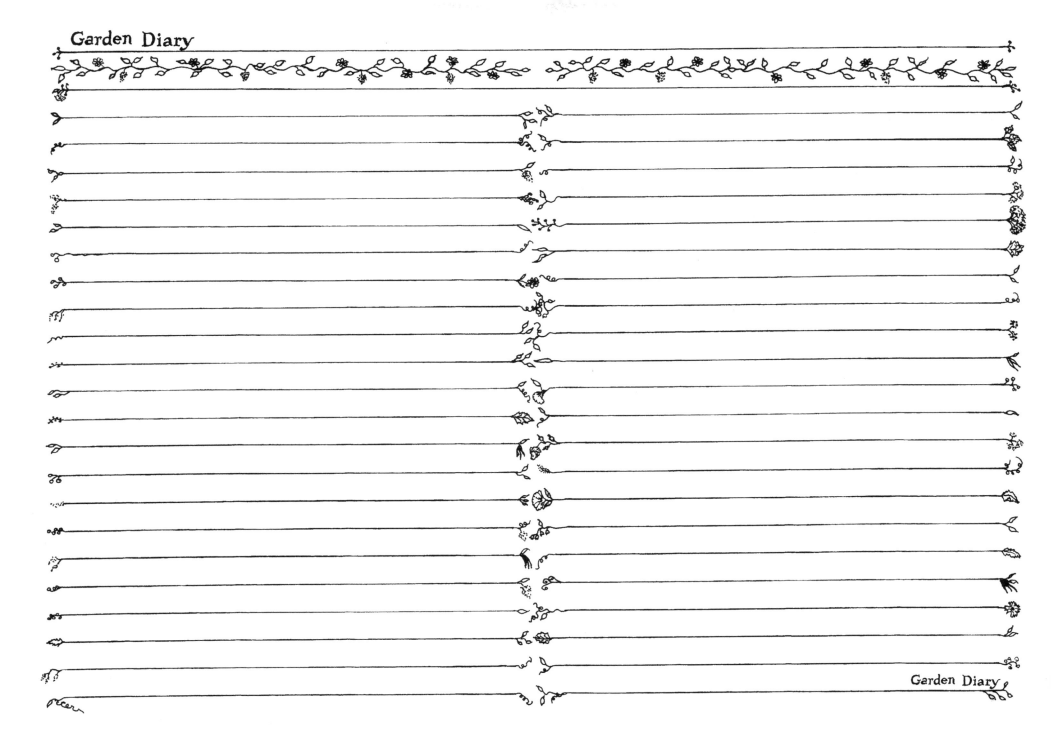

Garden Diary

Garden Diary

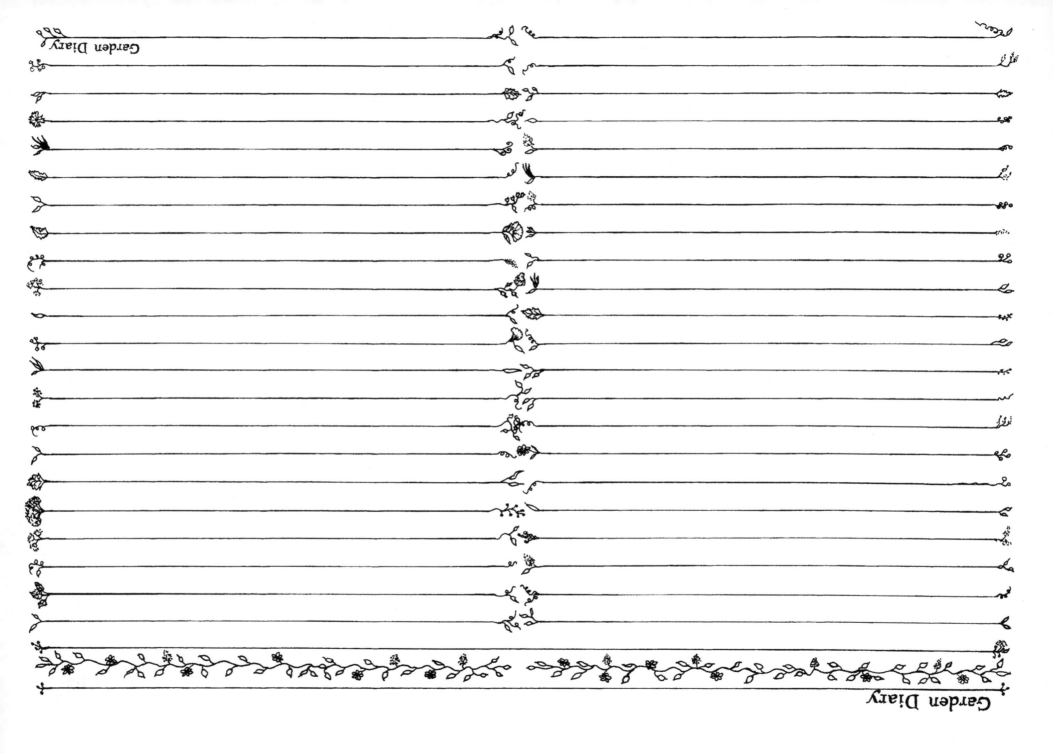

Garden Diary

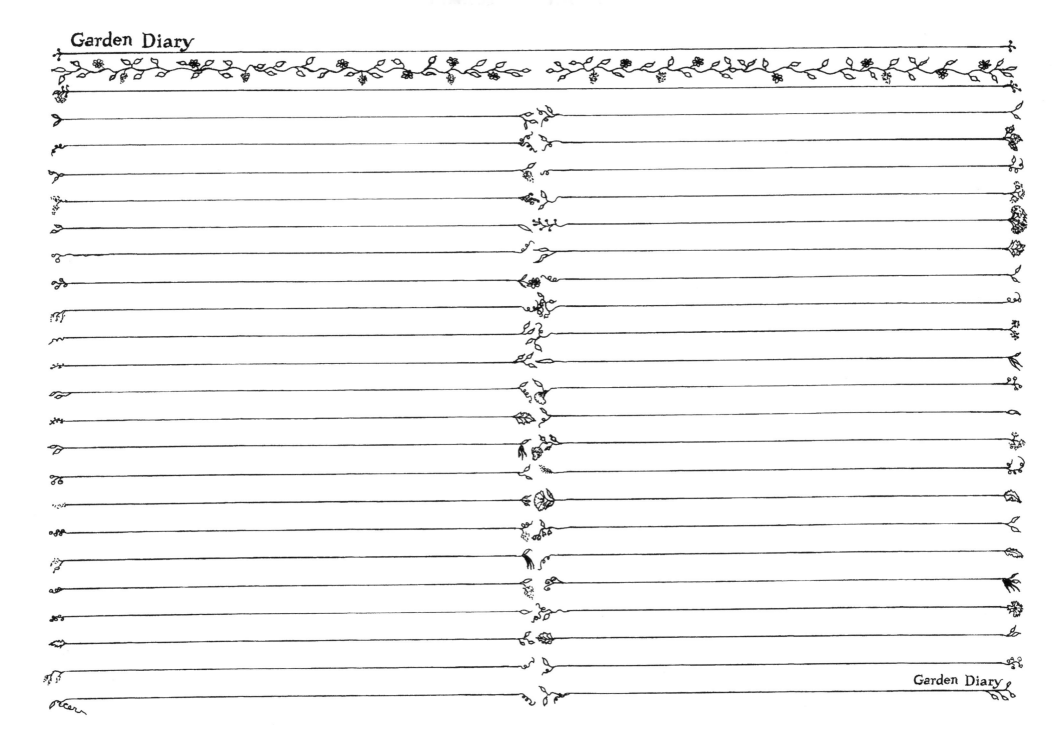

Garden Diary

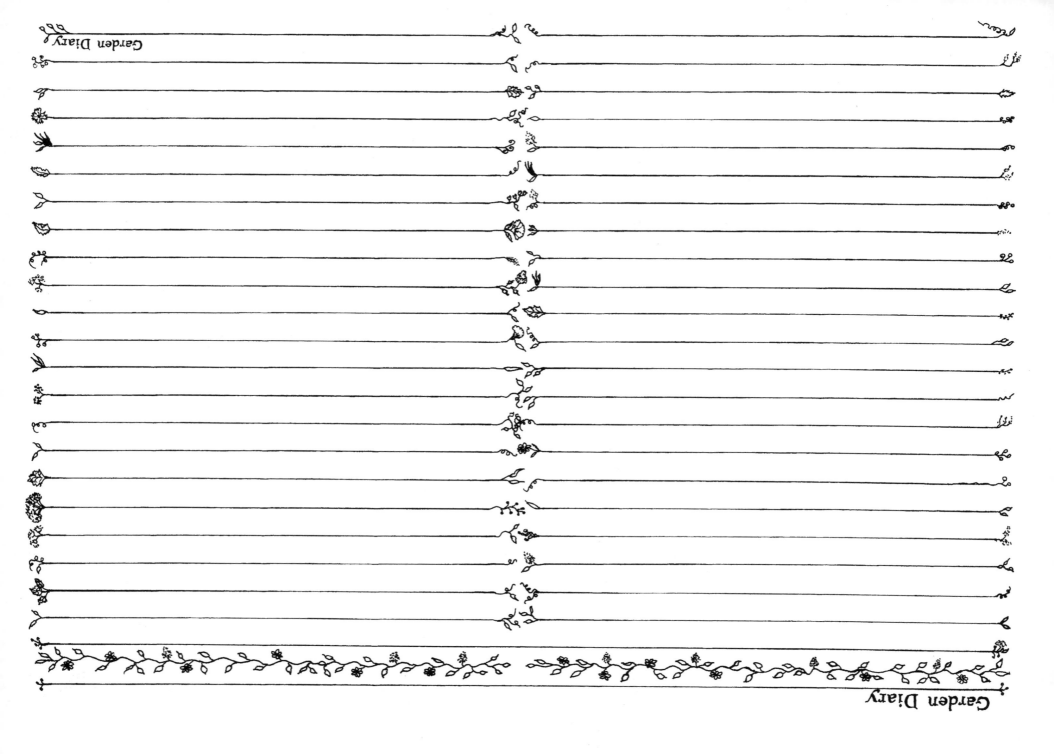

Garden Diary

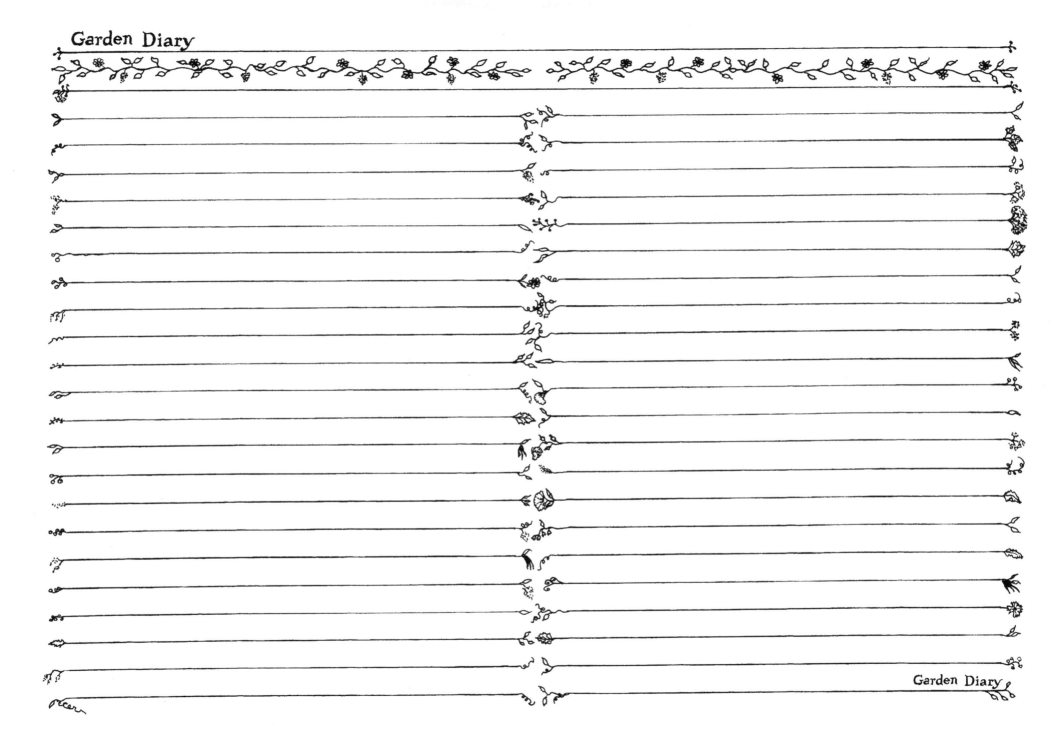

Garden Diary

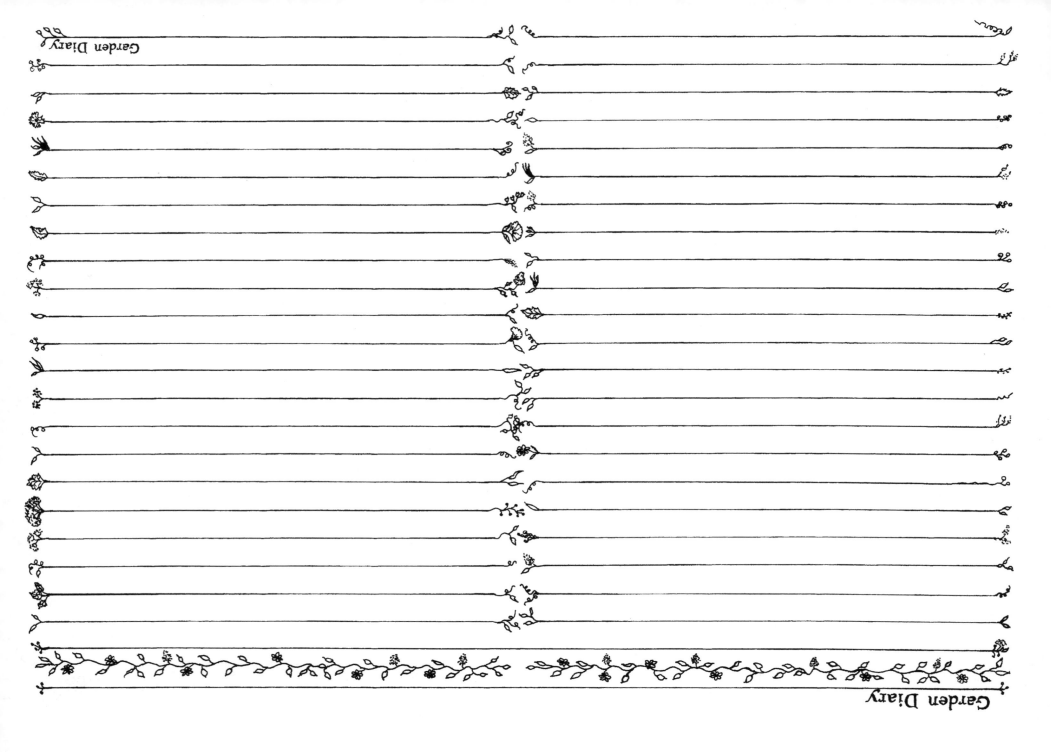

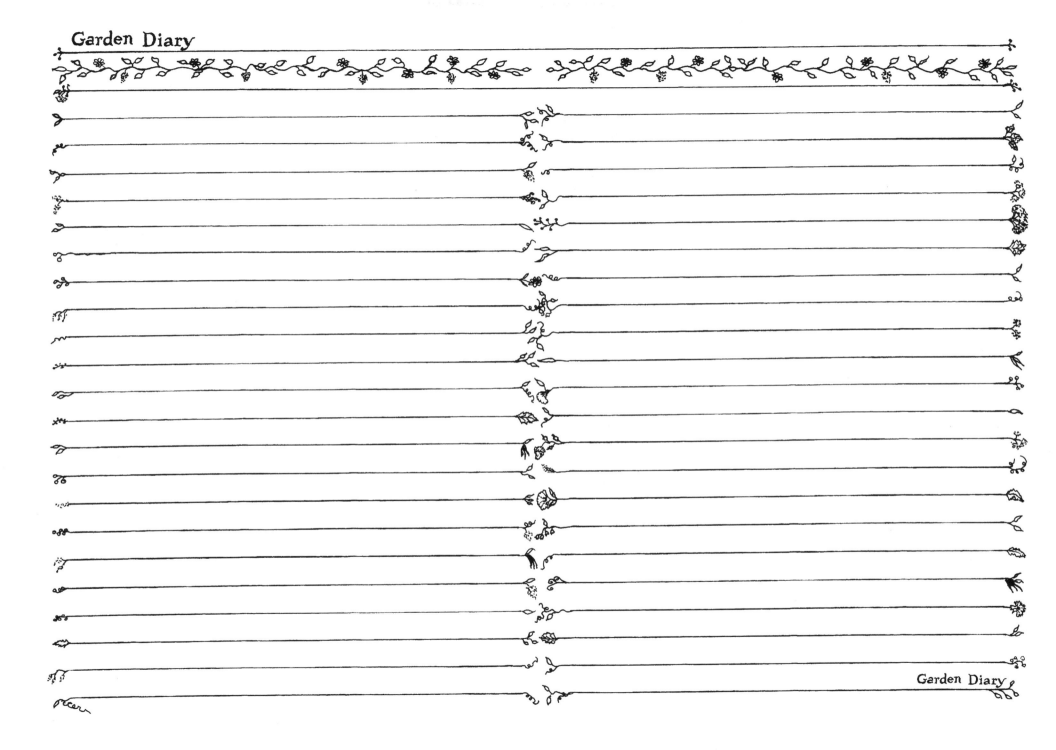

Garden Diary

Garden Diary

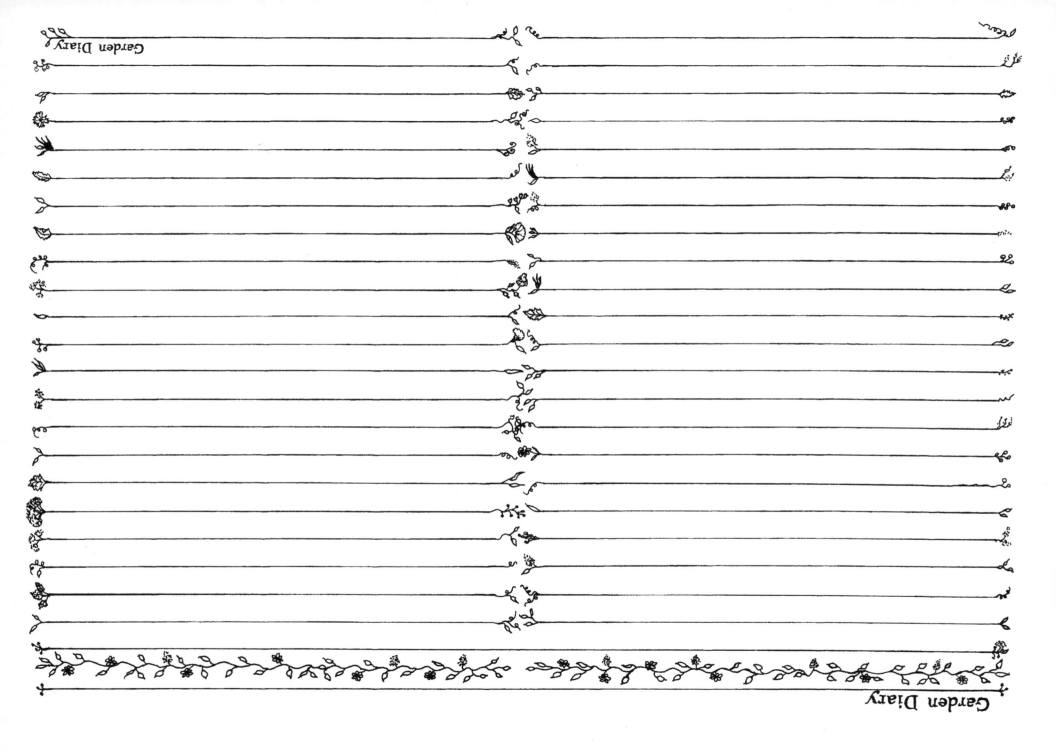

Garden Diary

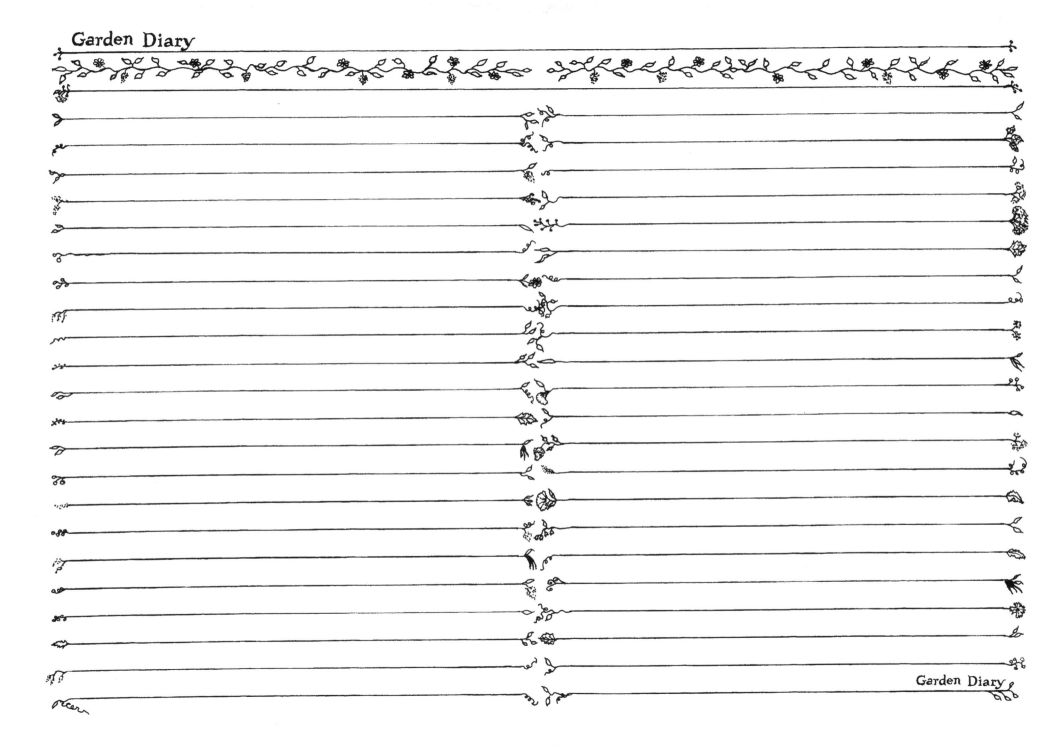

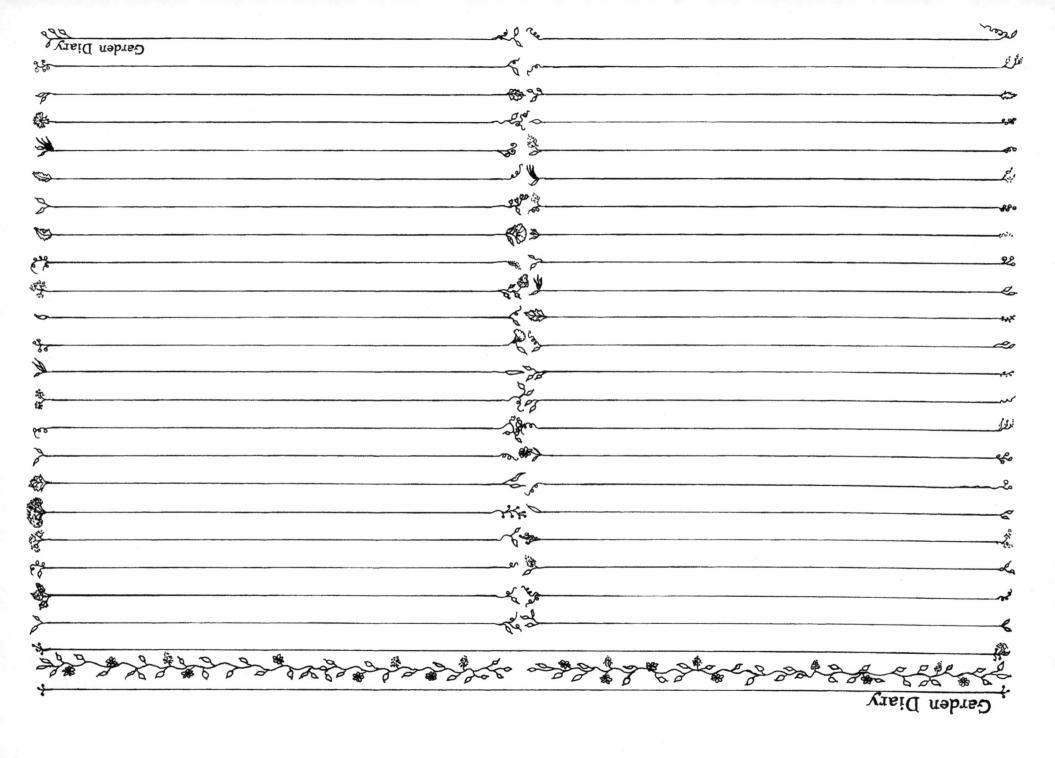

Garden Diary

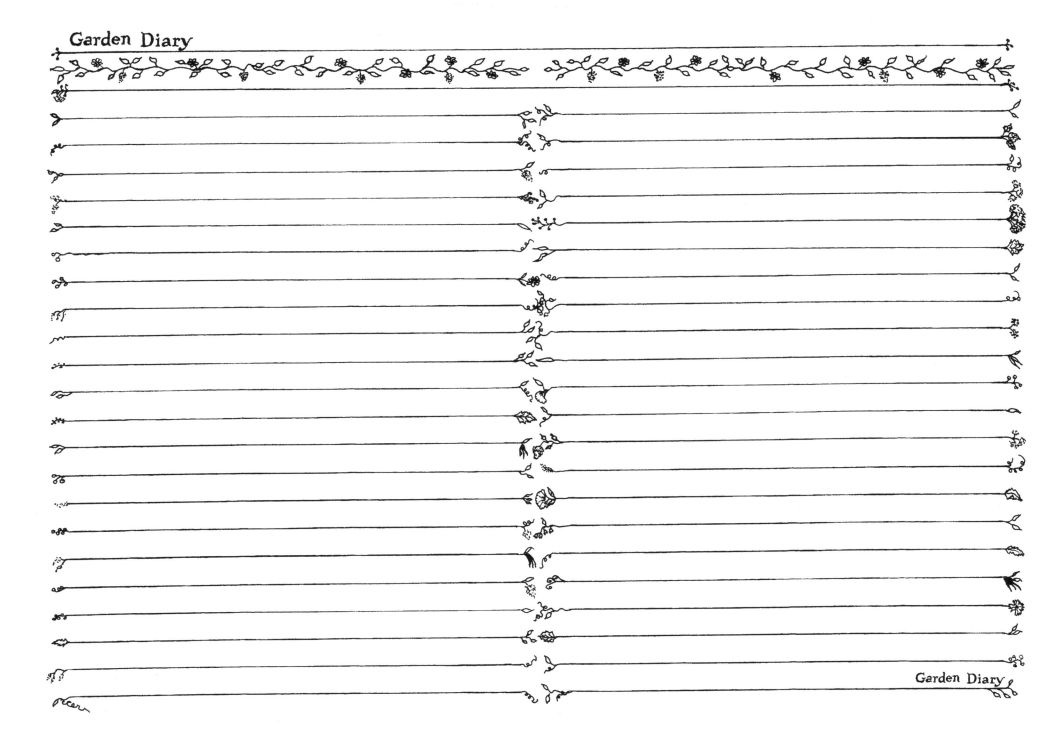

Garden Diary

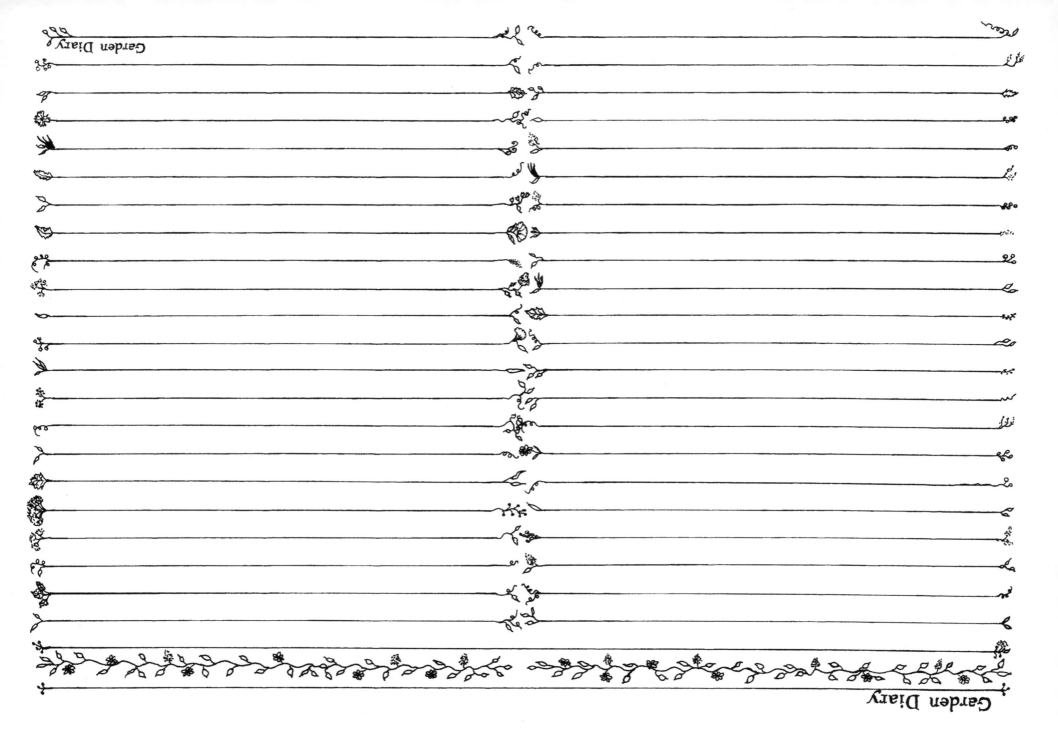

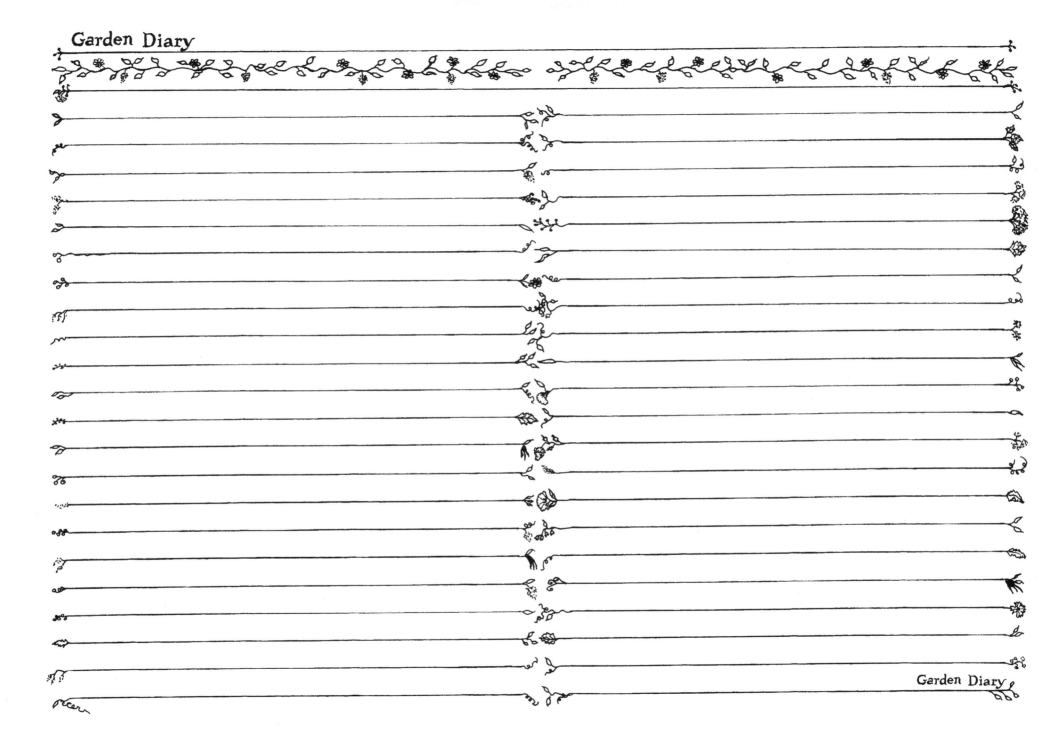

Garden Diary

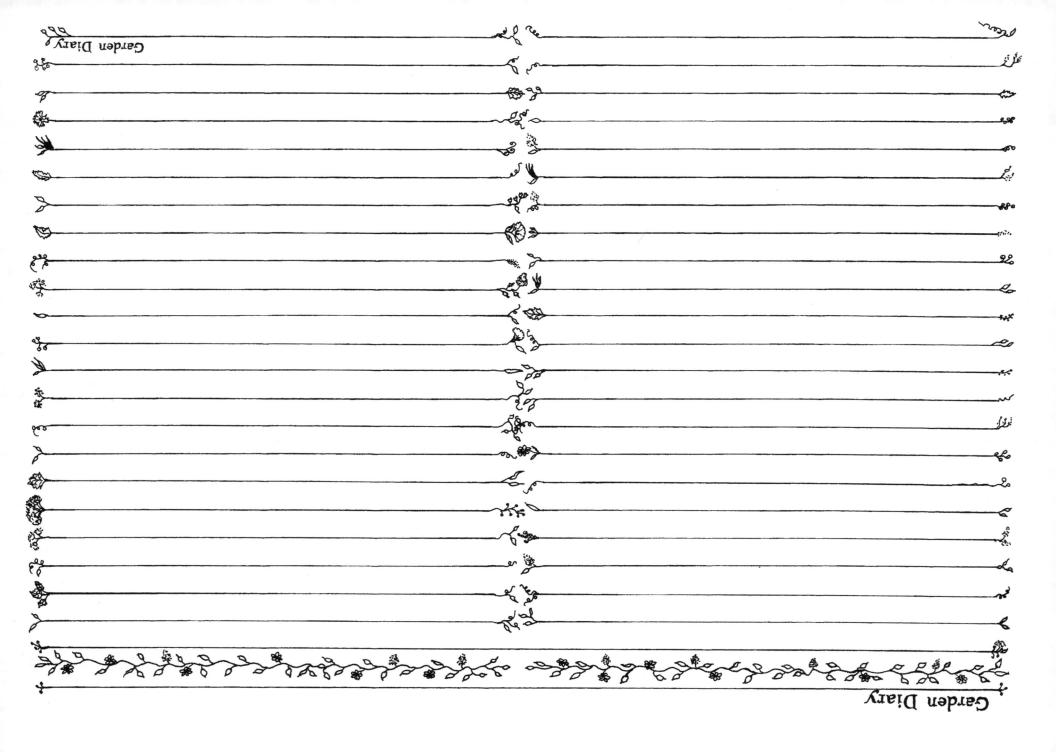

Garden Diary

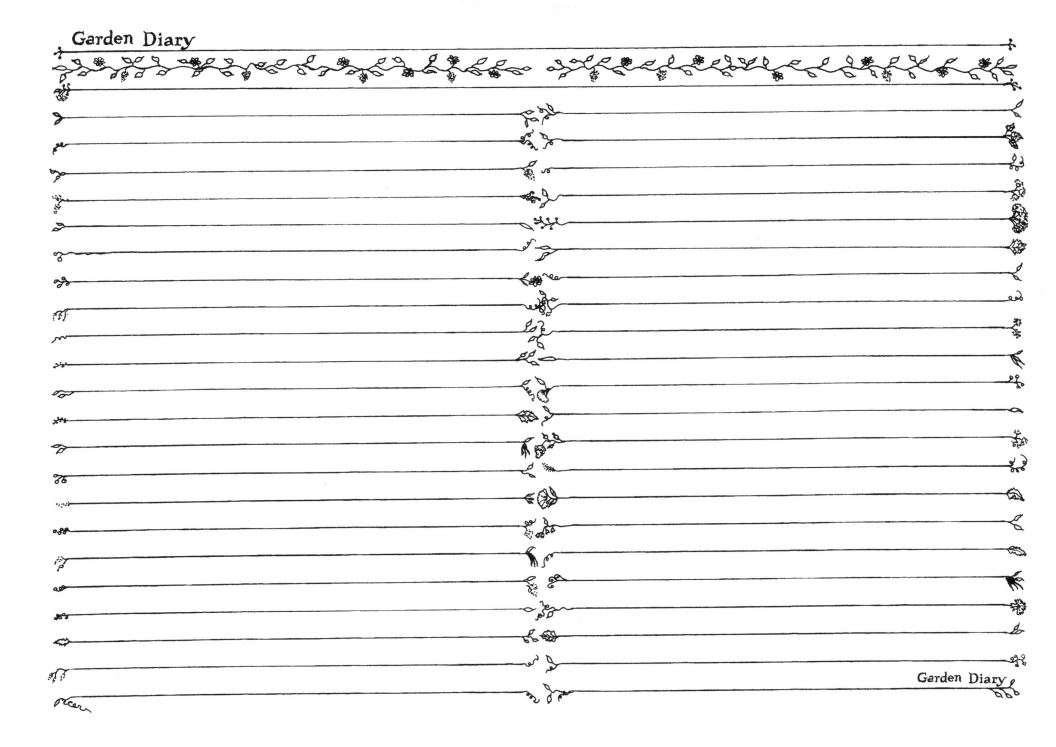

Garden Diary

Garden Diary

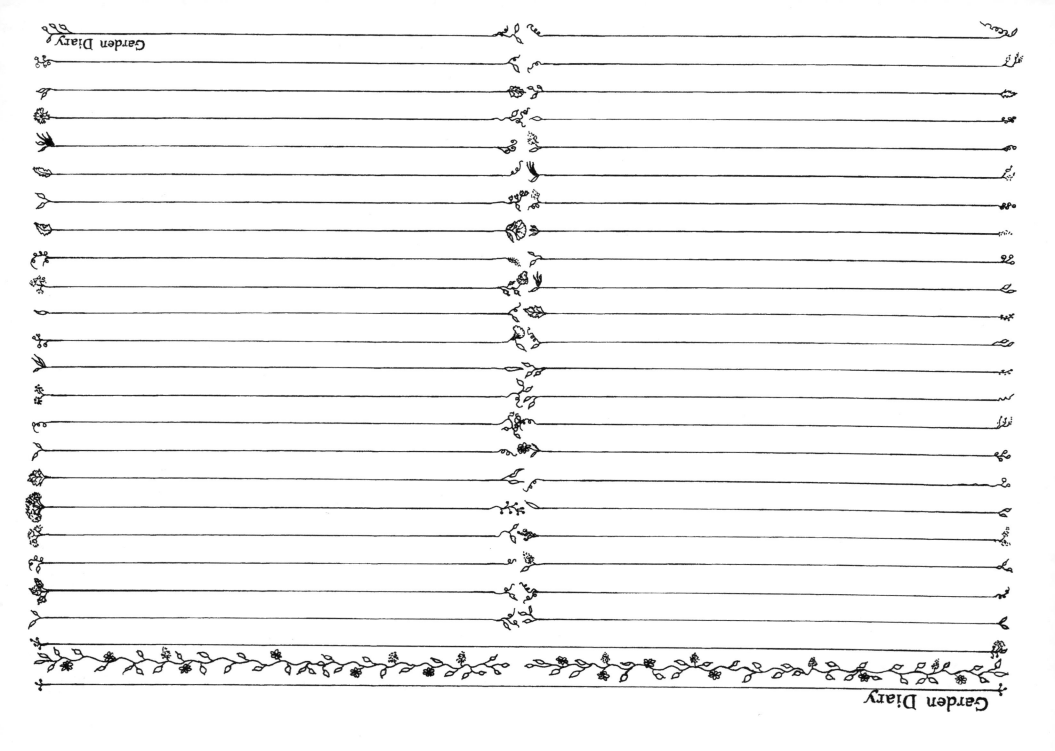

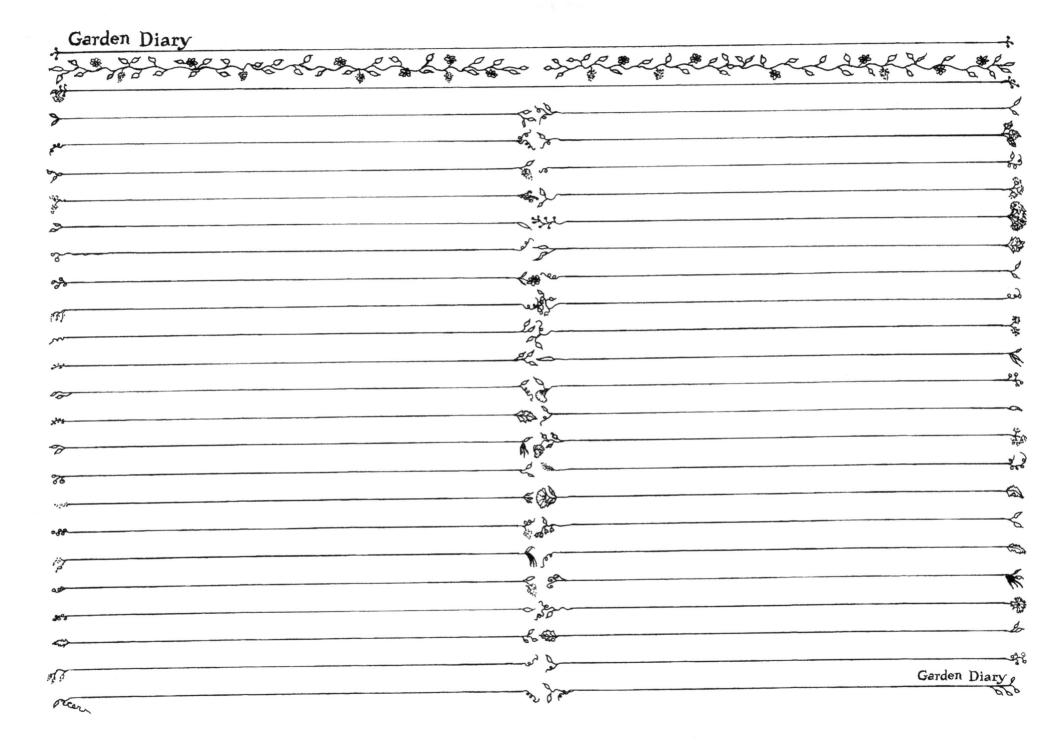

Garden Diary

Garden Diary

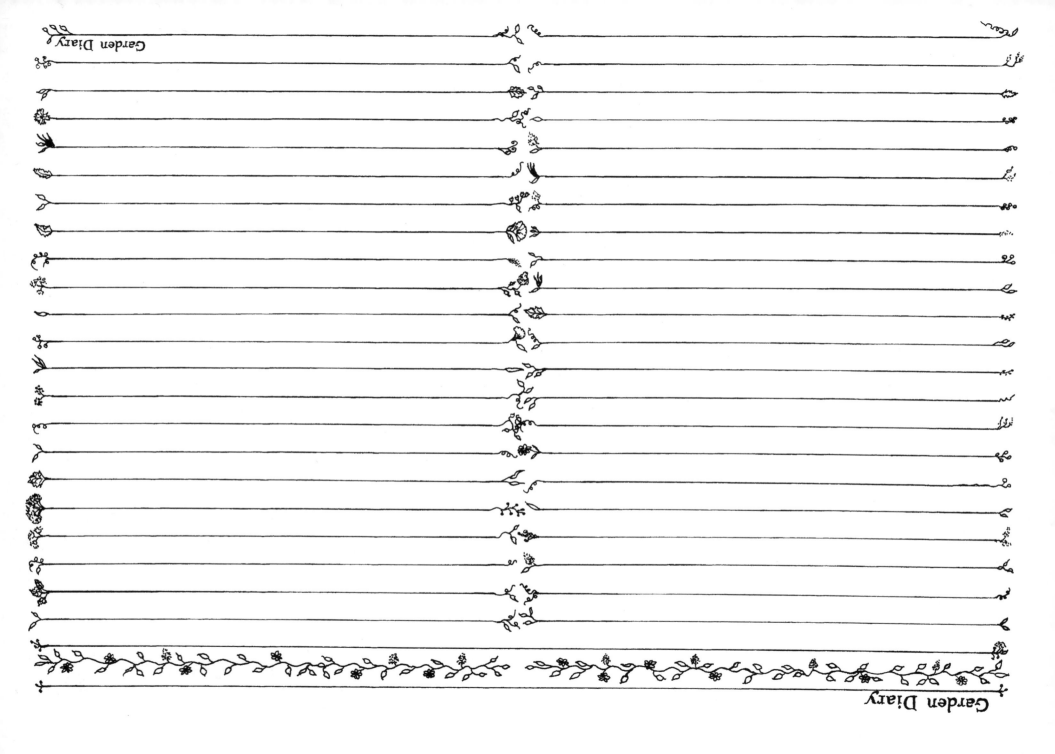

Garden Diary

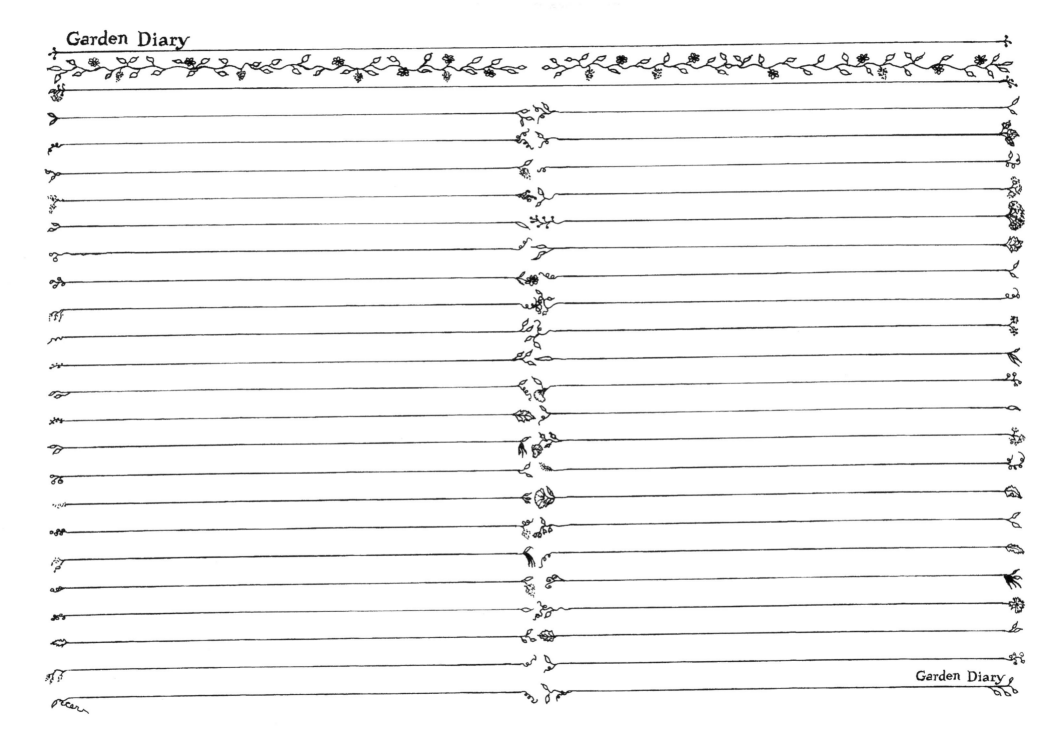

Garden Diary

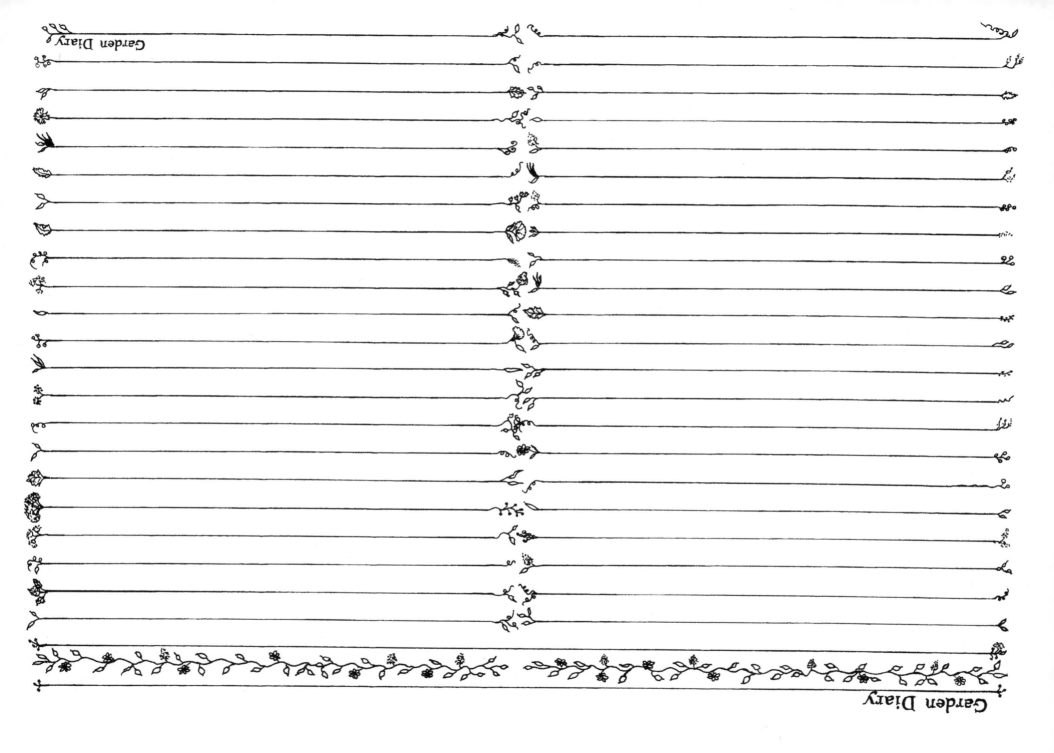

Garden Diary

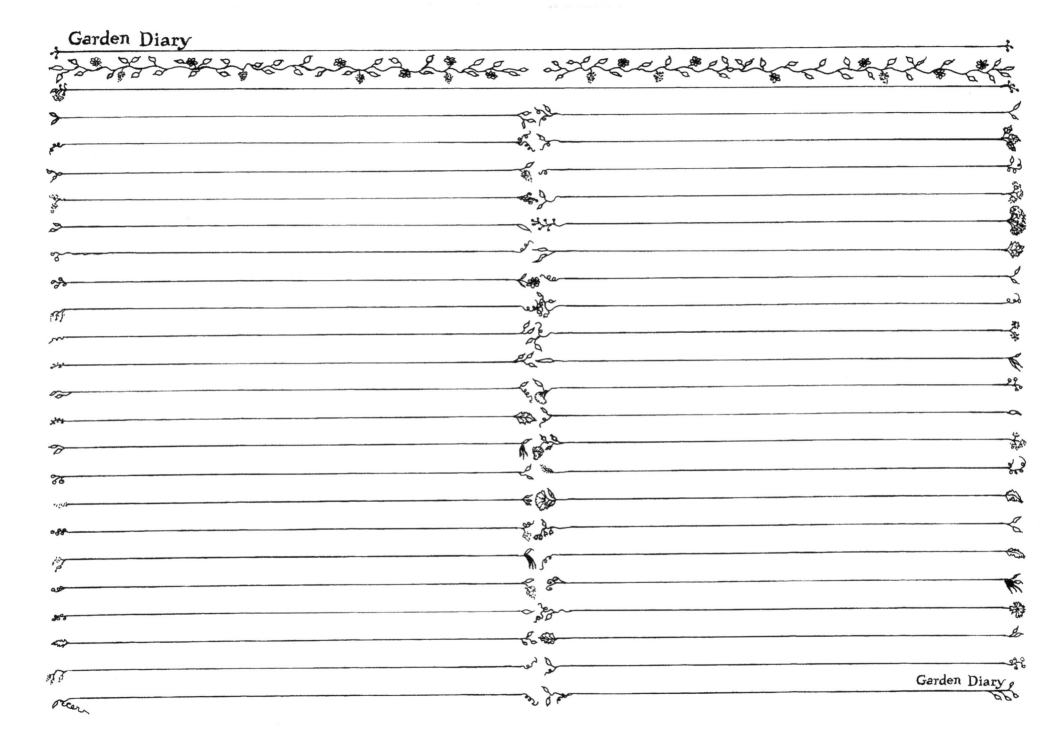

Garden Diary

Garden Diary

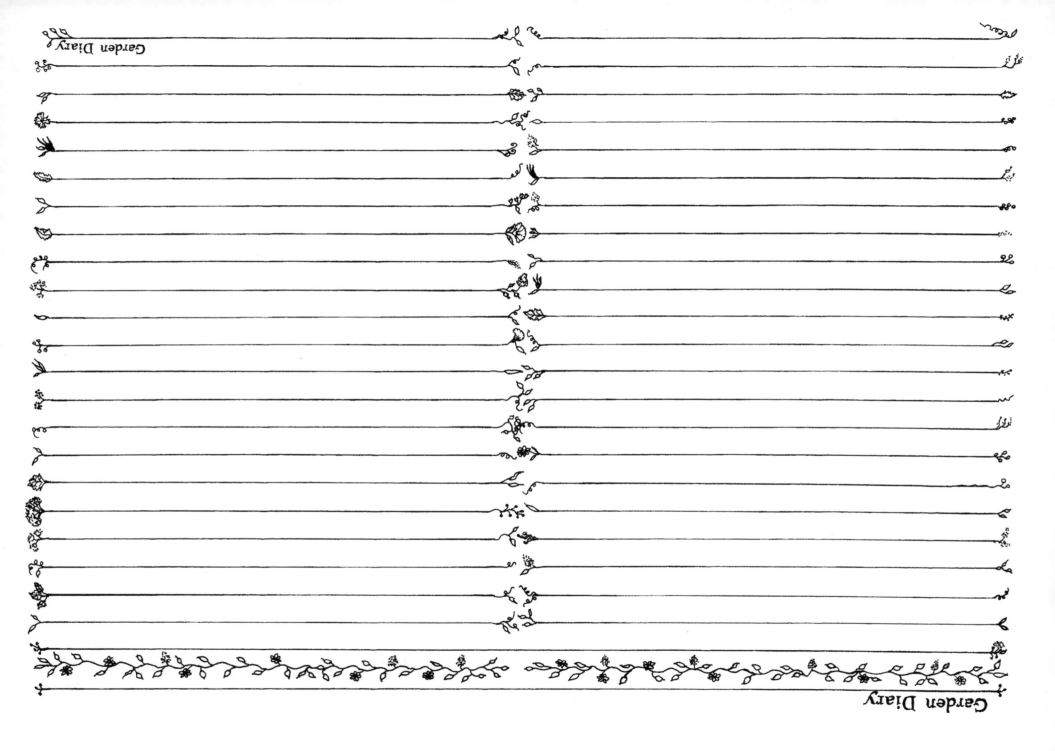

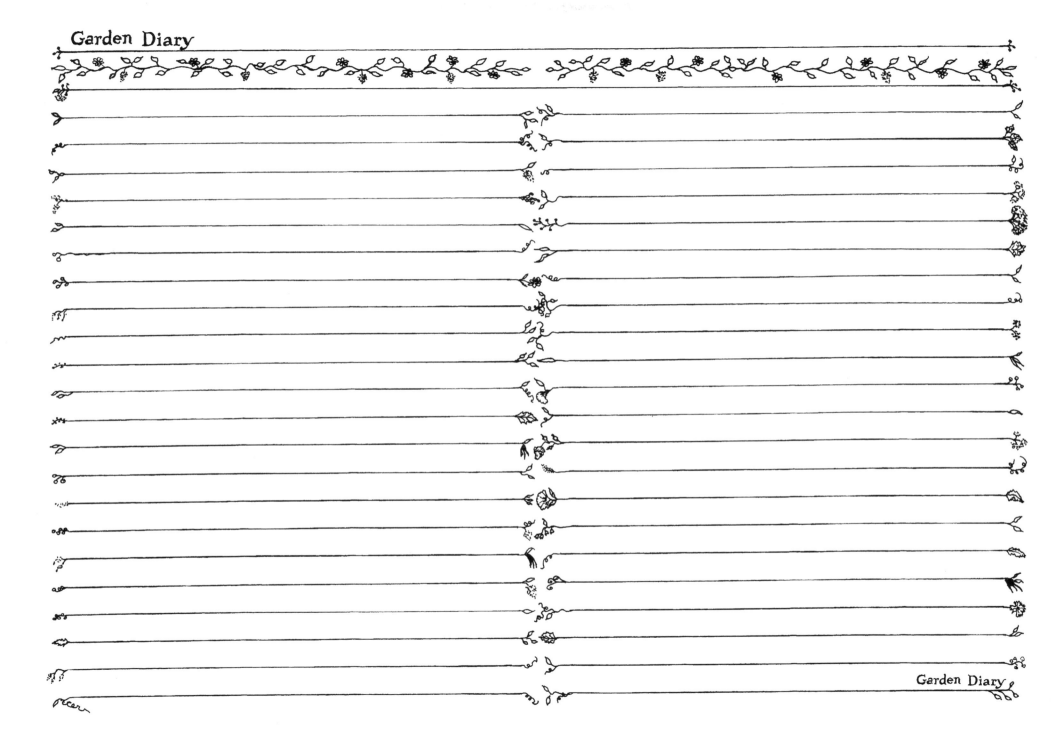

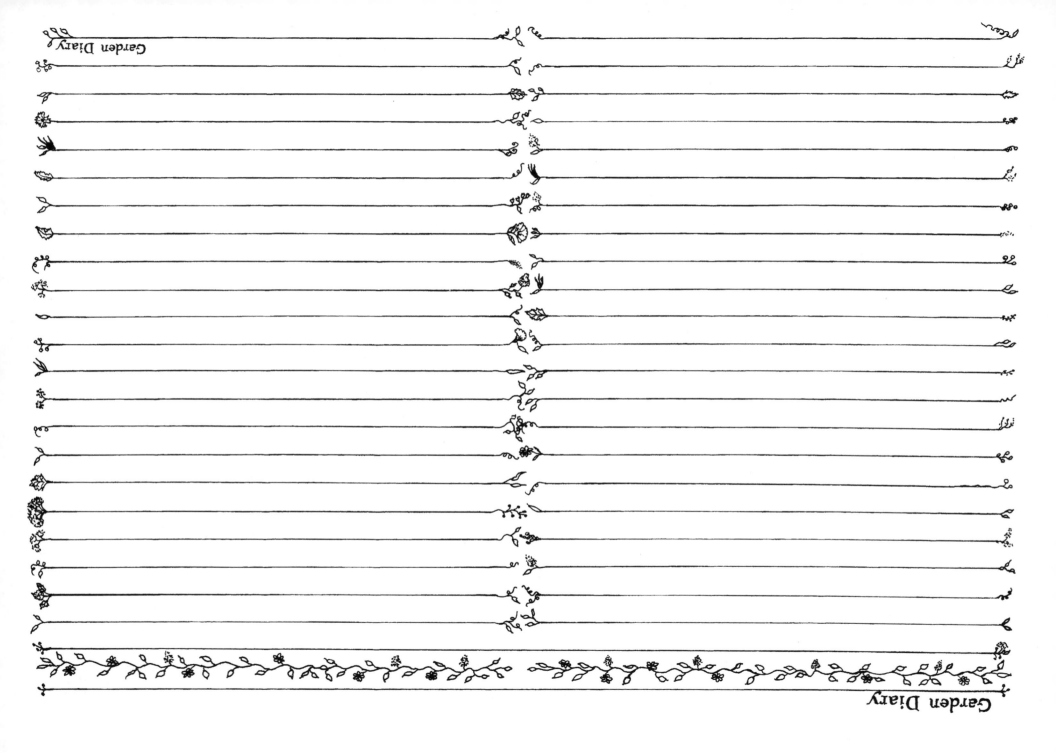

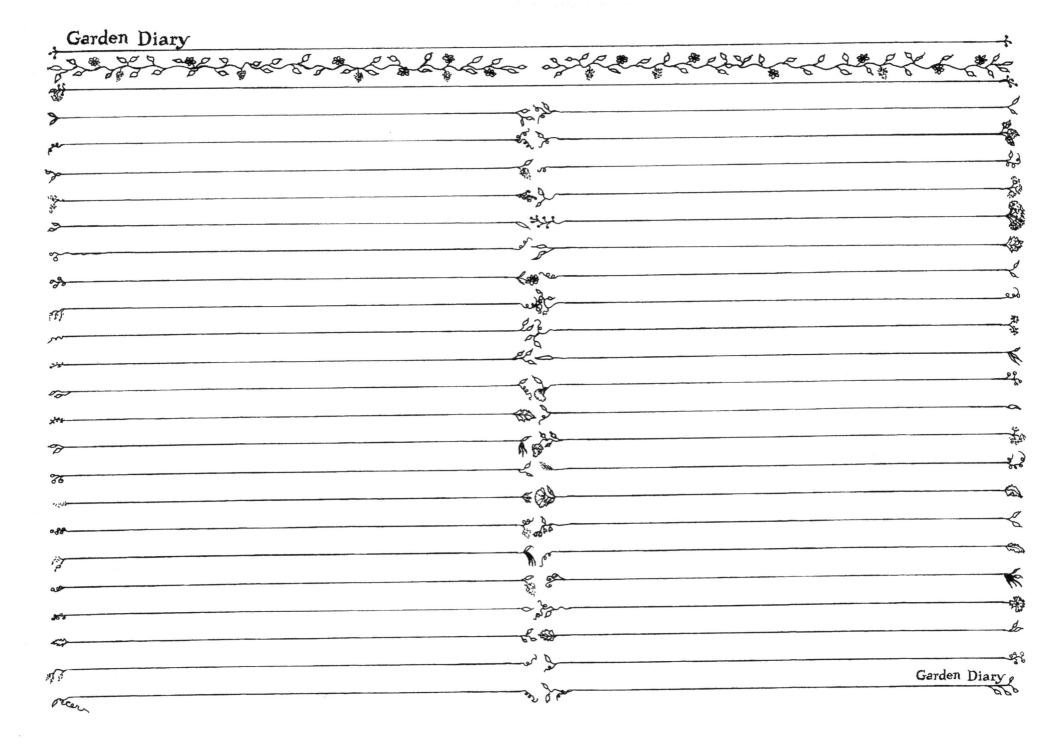

Garden Diary

Garden Diary

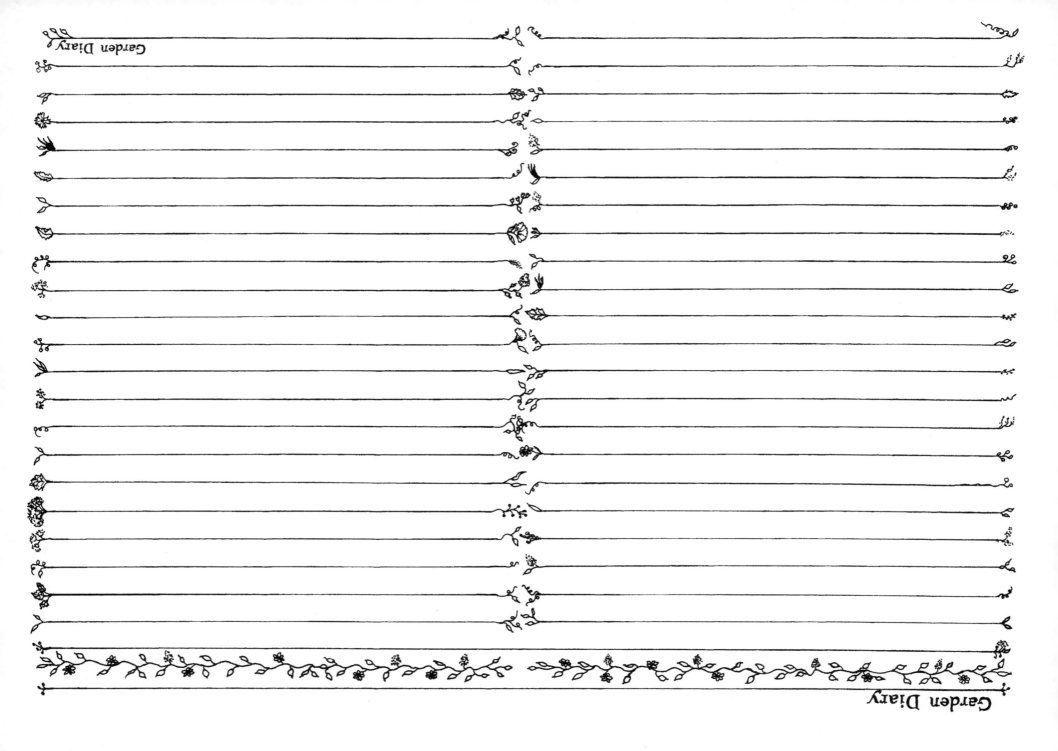

Garden Diary

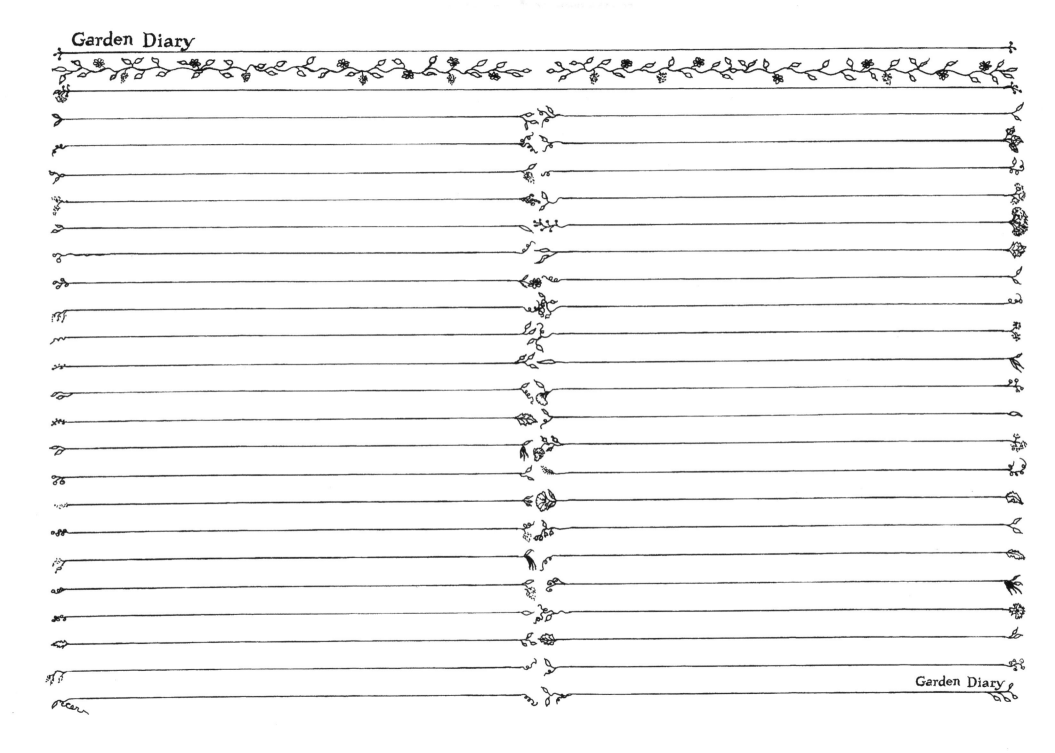

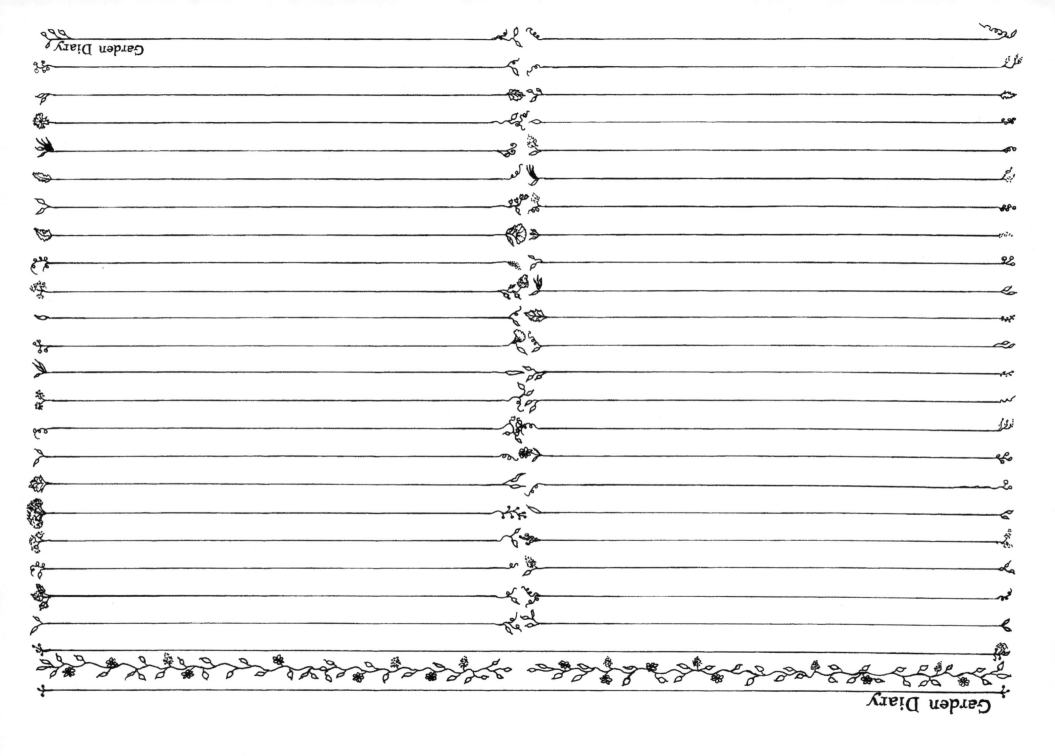
Garden Diary

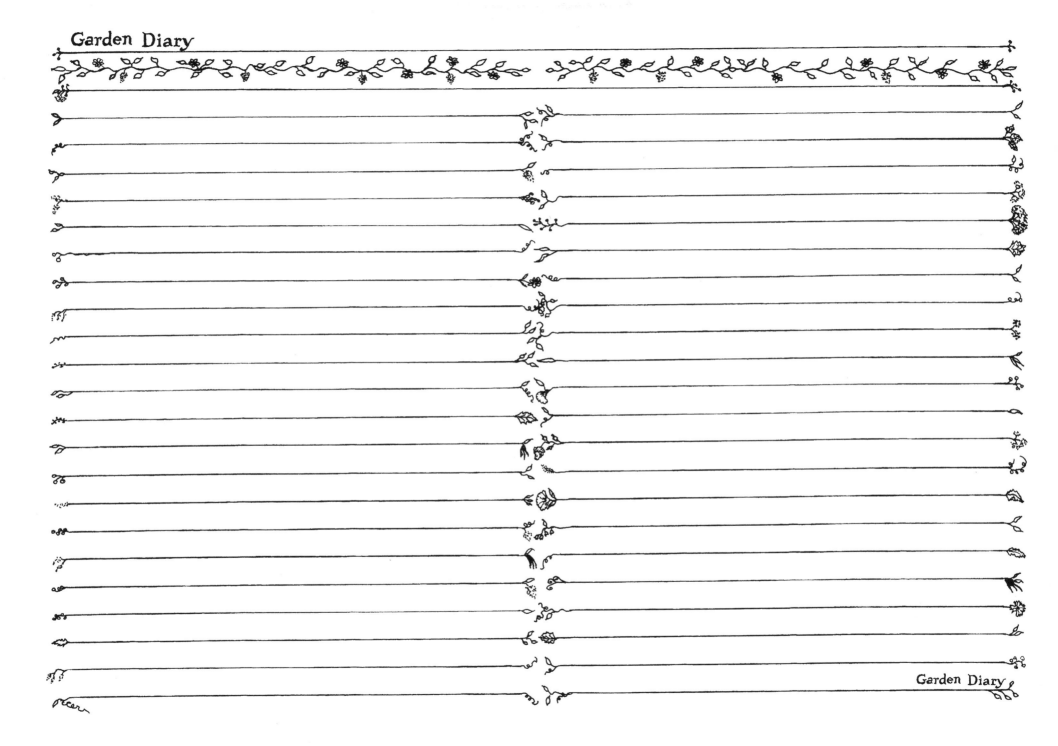

Garden Diary

Garden Diary

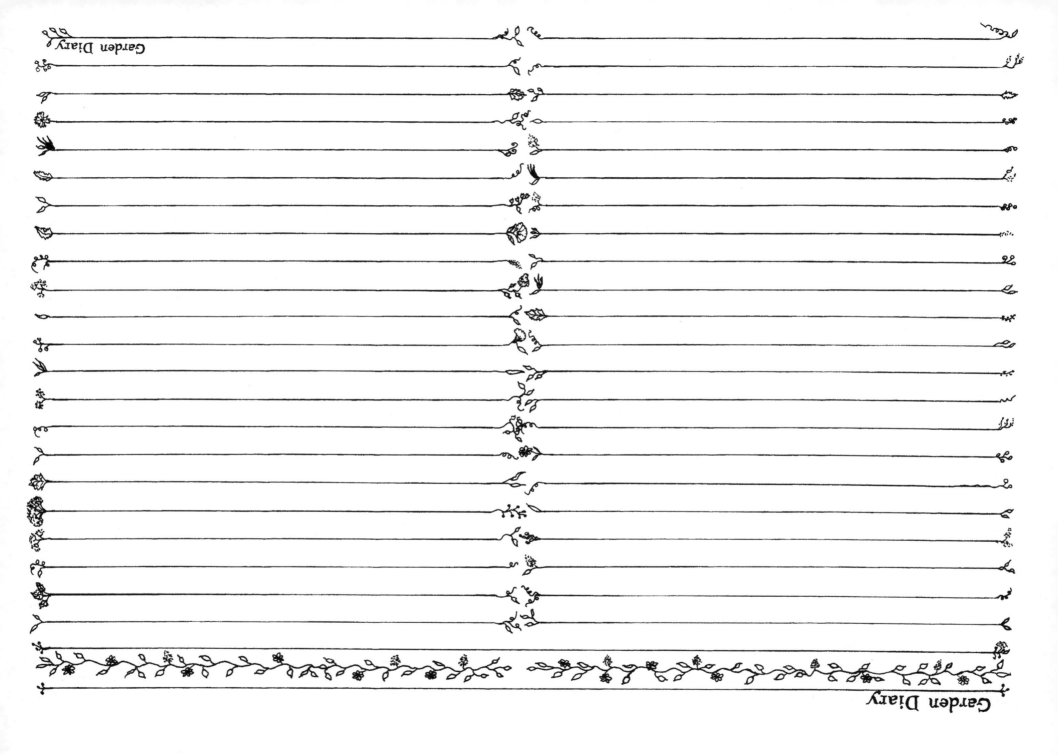

Garden Diary

Garden Diary

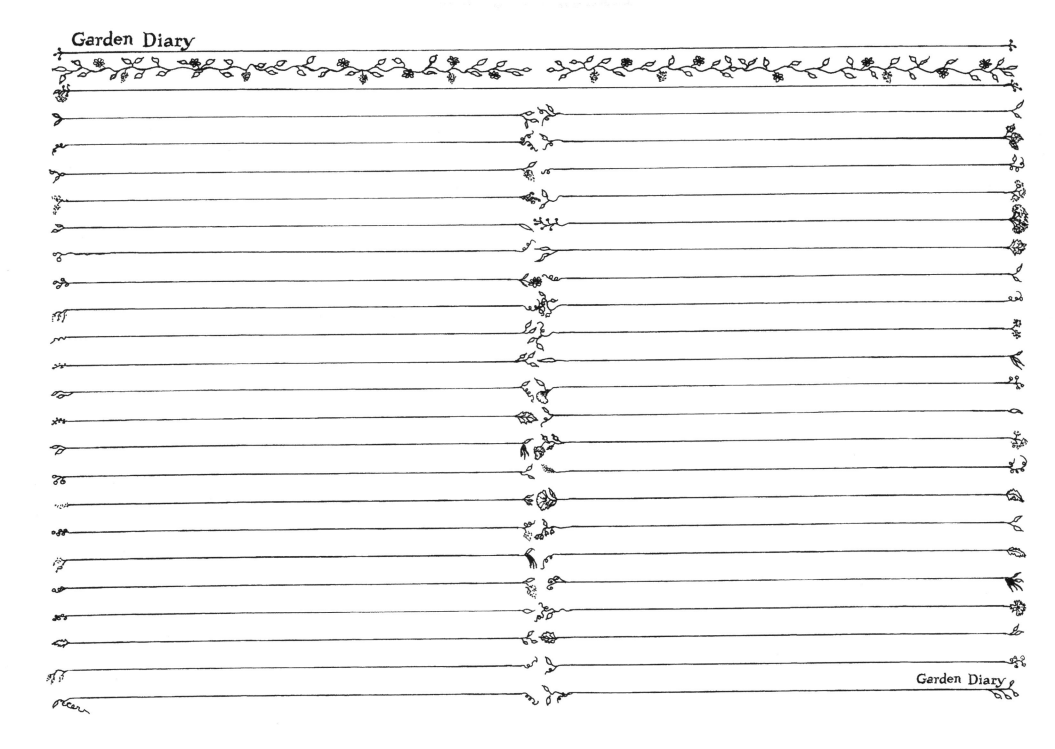

Garden Diary

Garden Diary

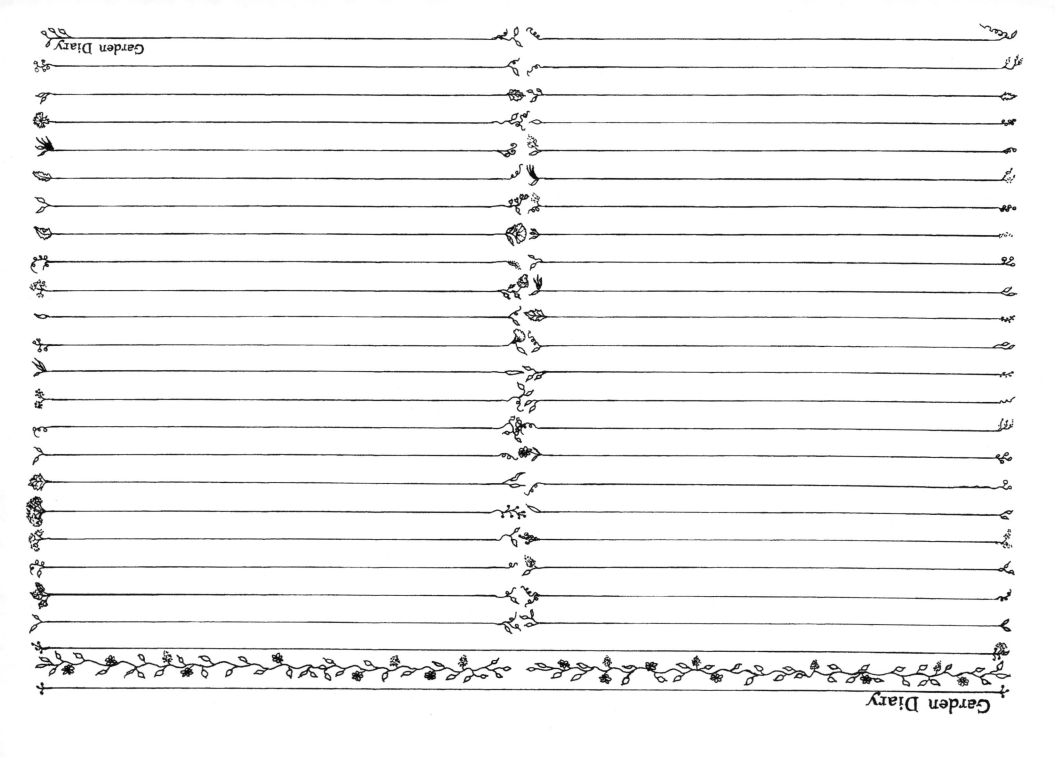

Garden Diary

Garden Diary

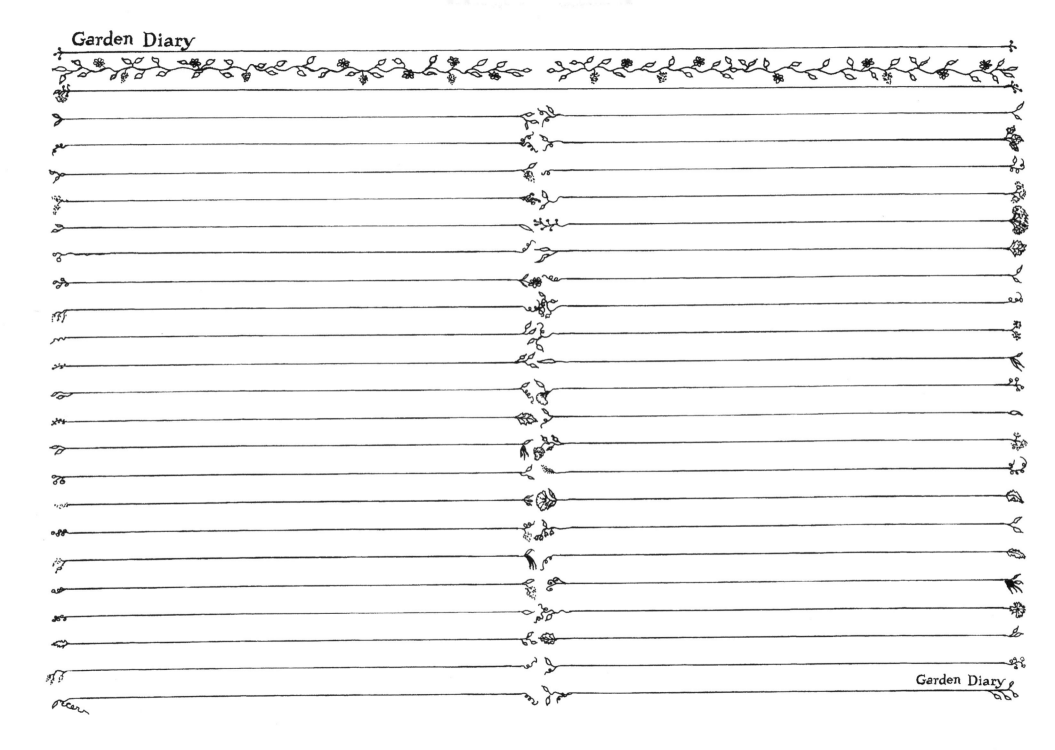

Garden Diary

Garden Diary

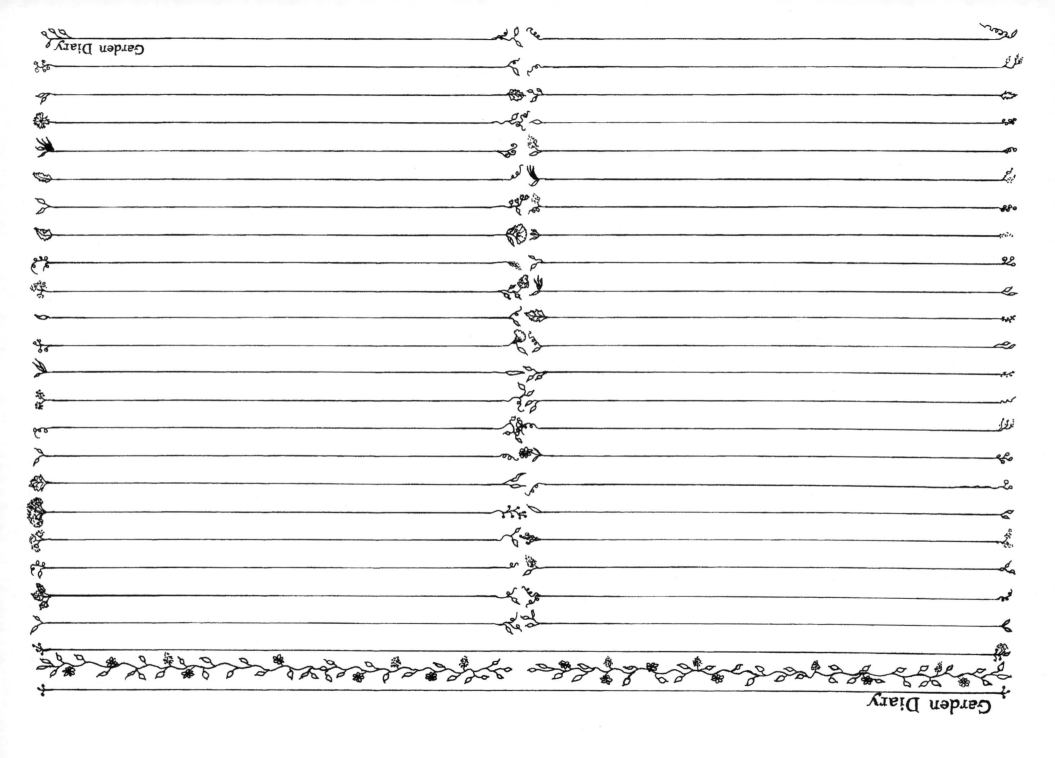

Garden Diary

Garden Diary

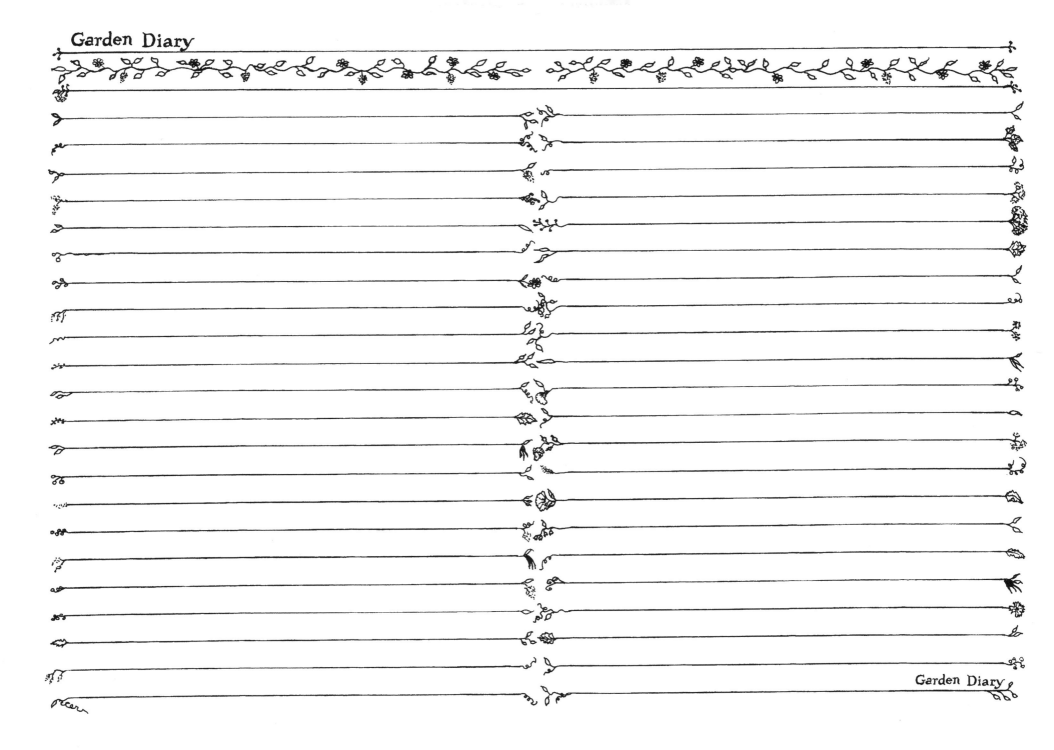

Garden Diary

Garden Diary

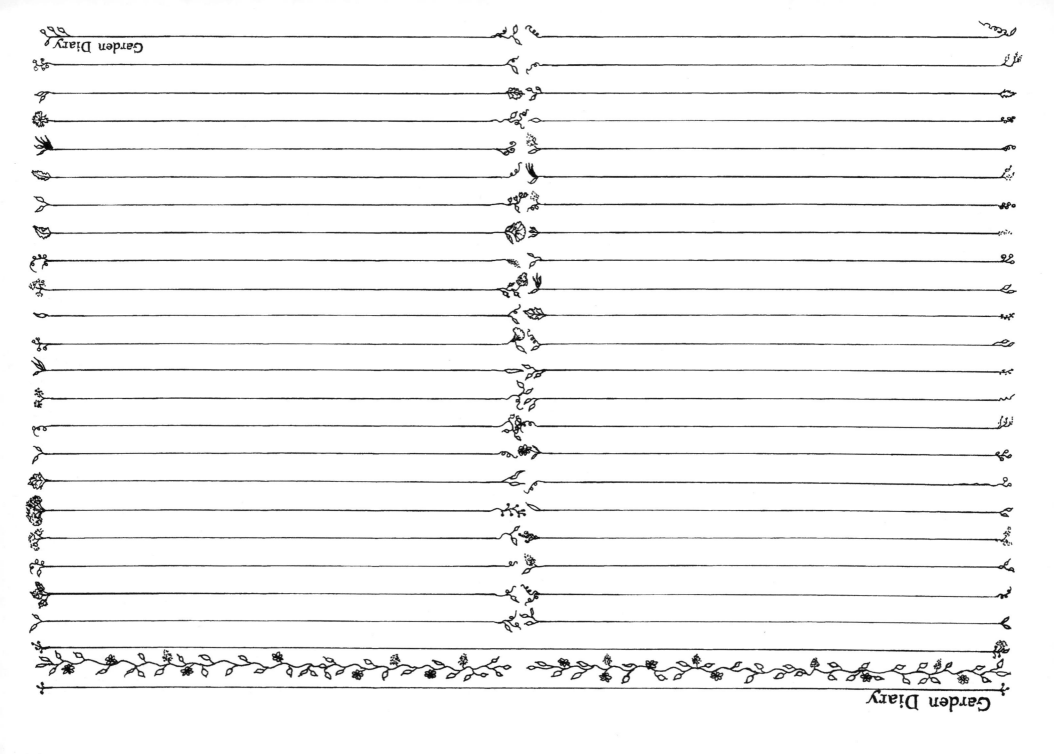

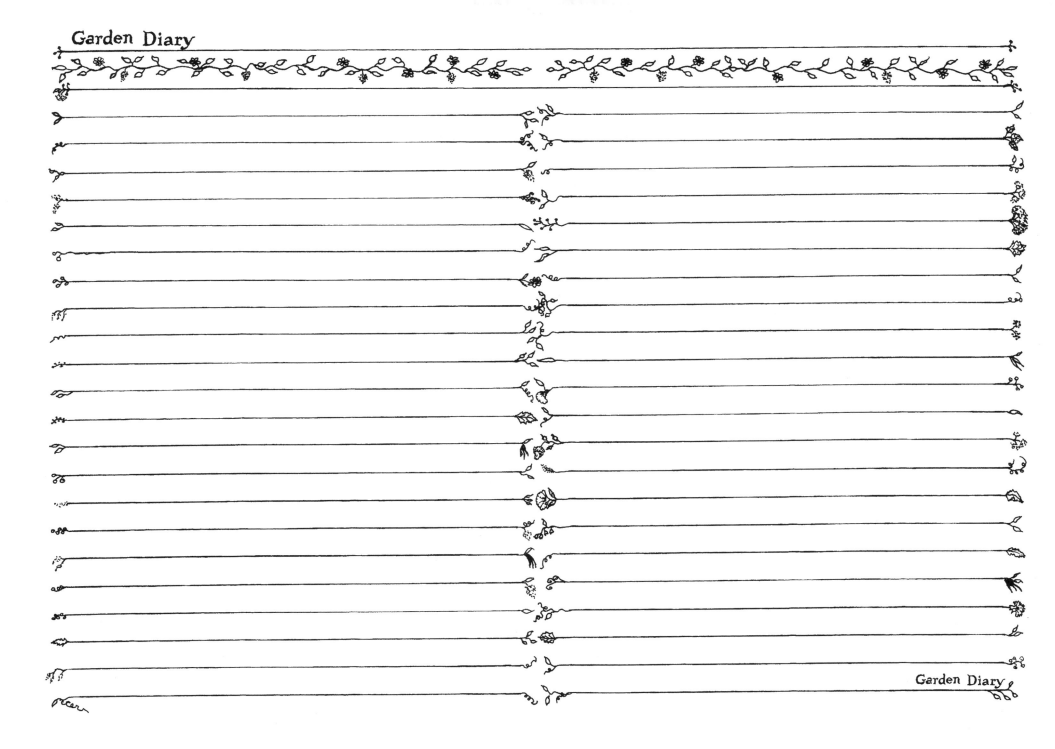

Garden Diary

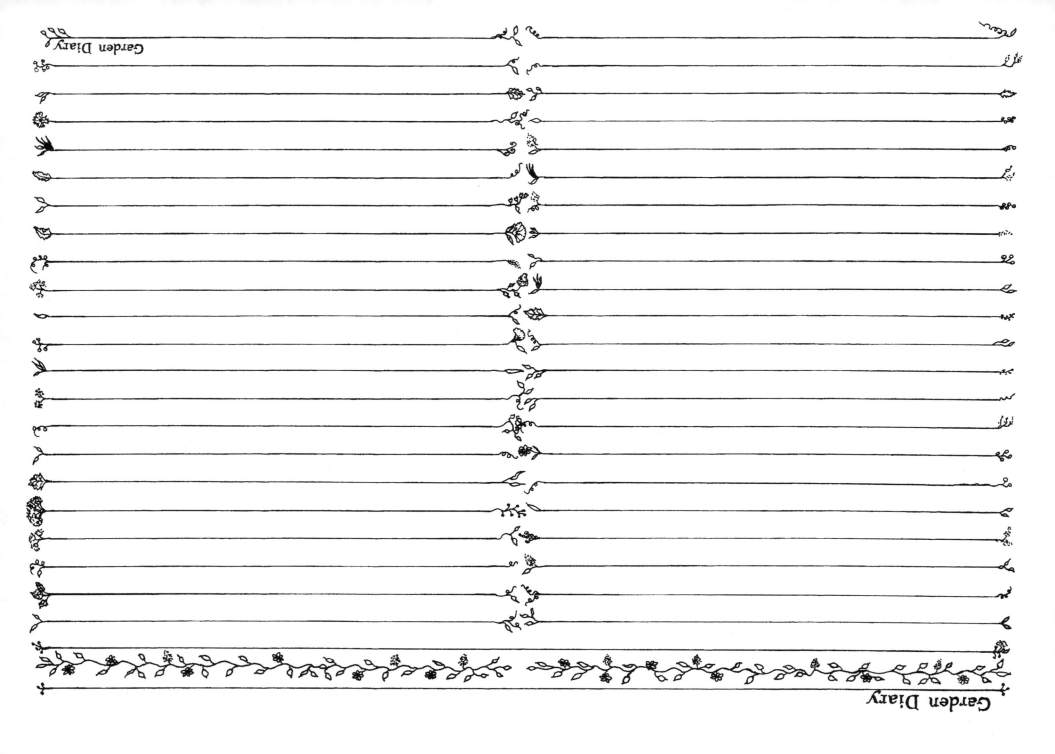

Garden Diary

Garden Diary

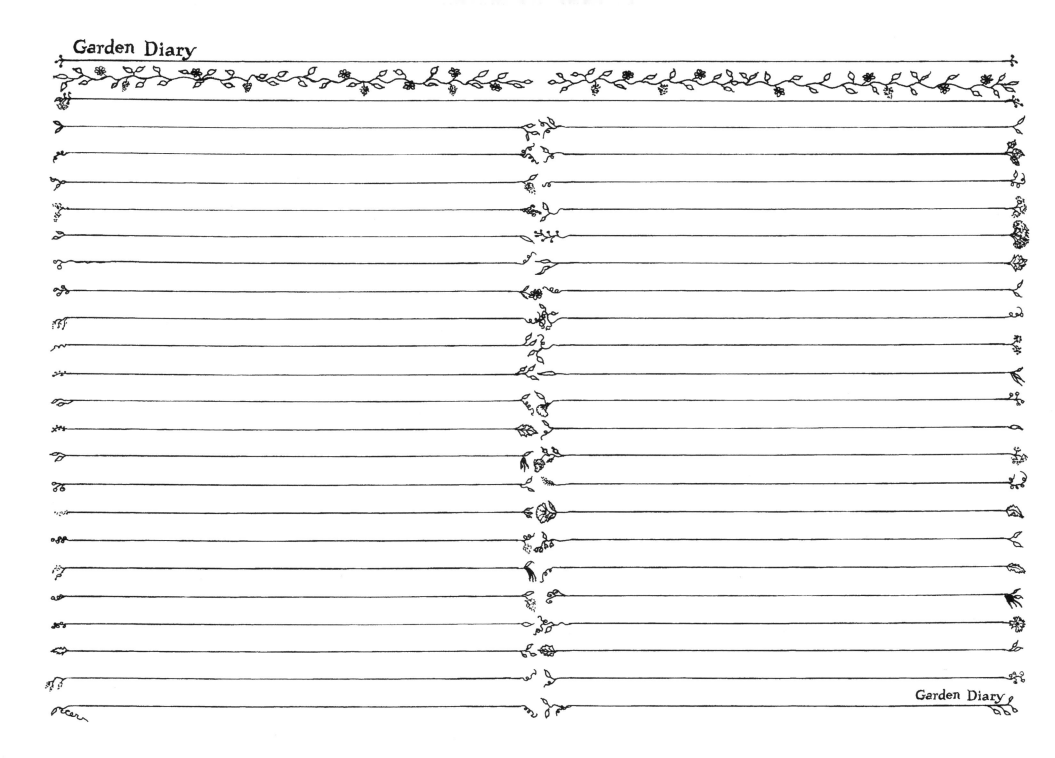

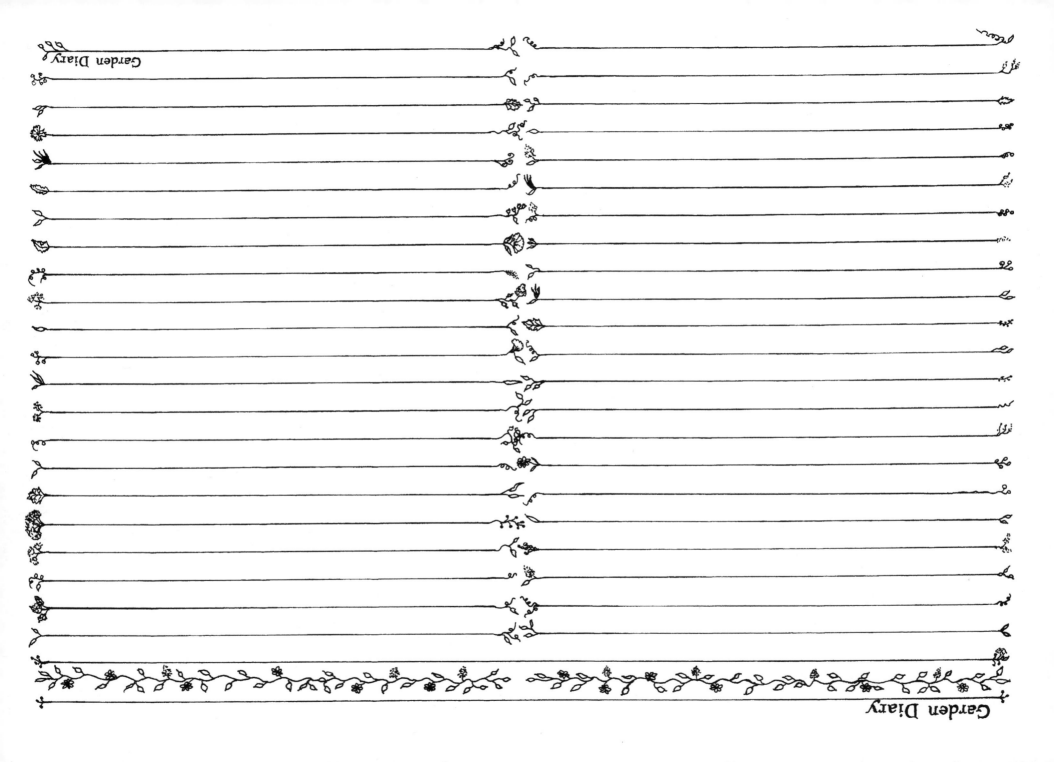

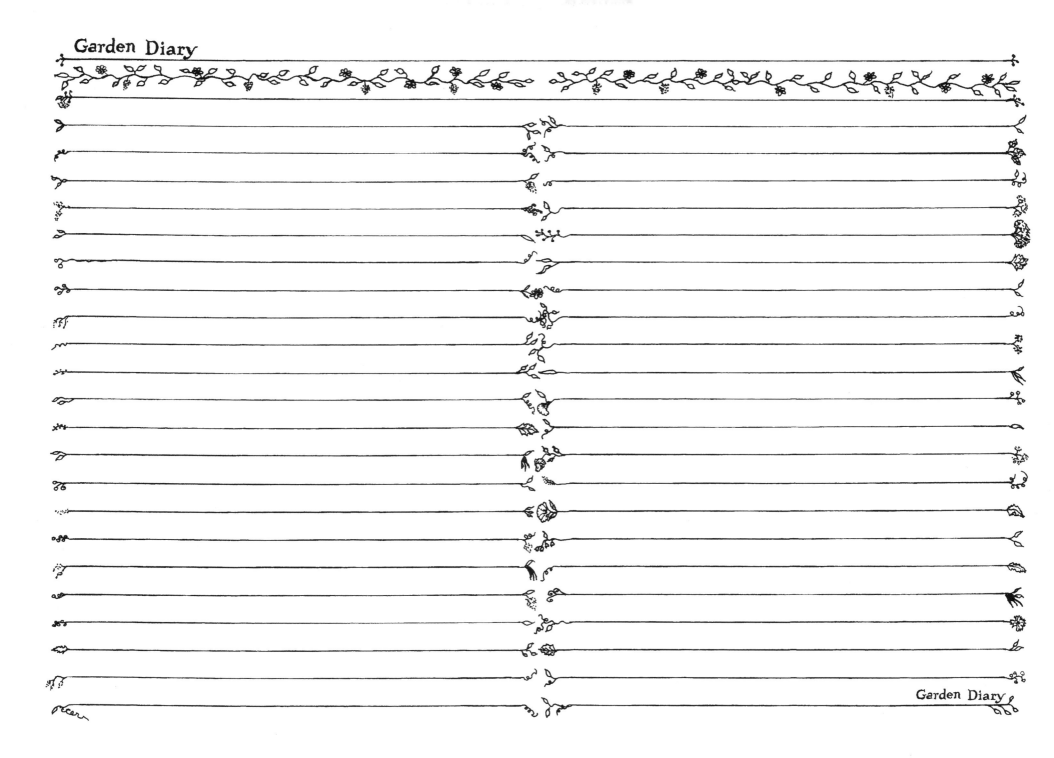

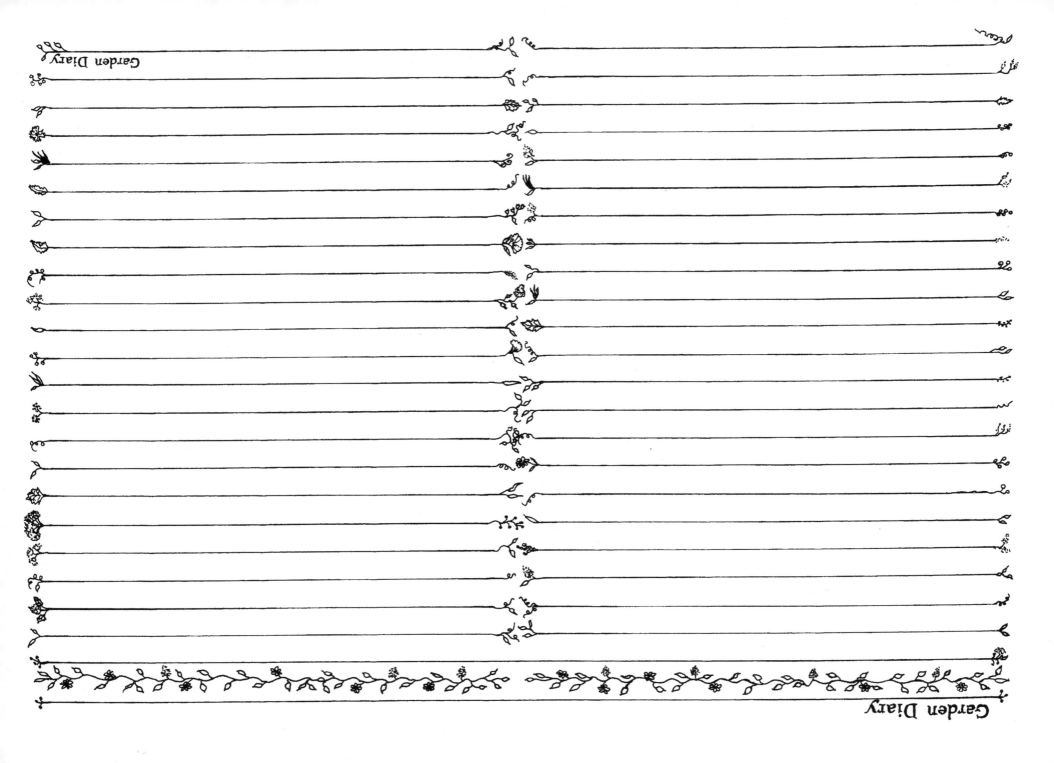

Garden Diary

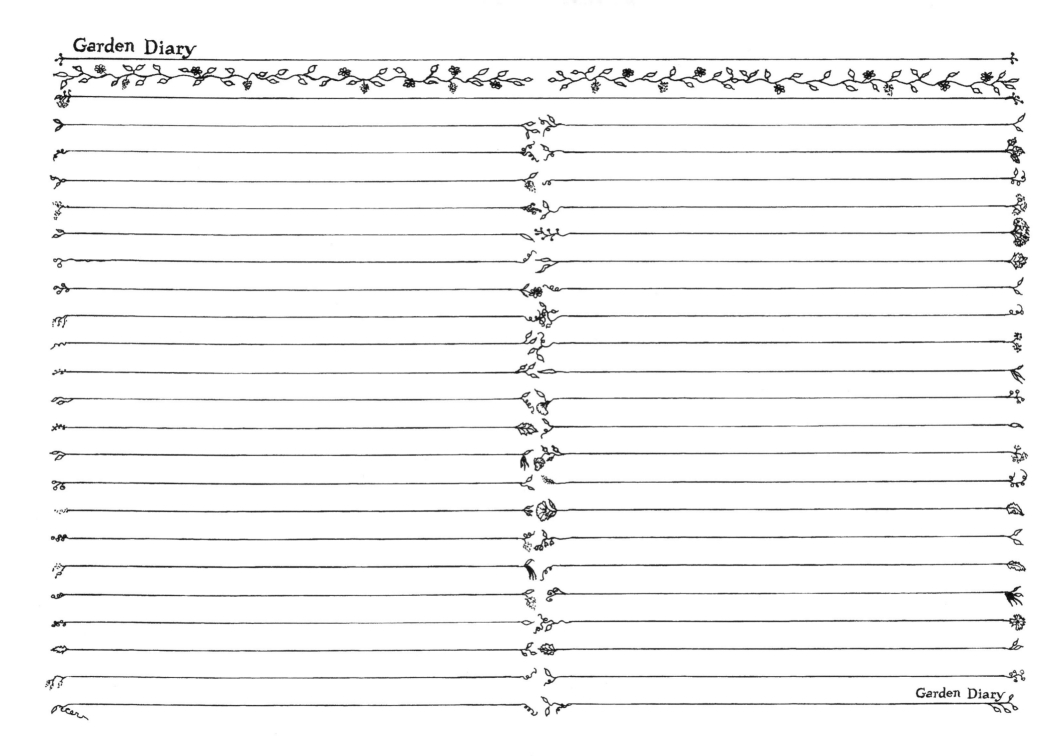

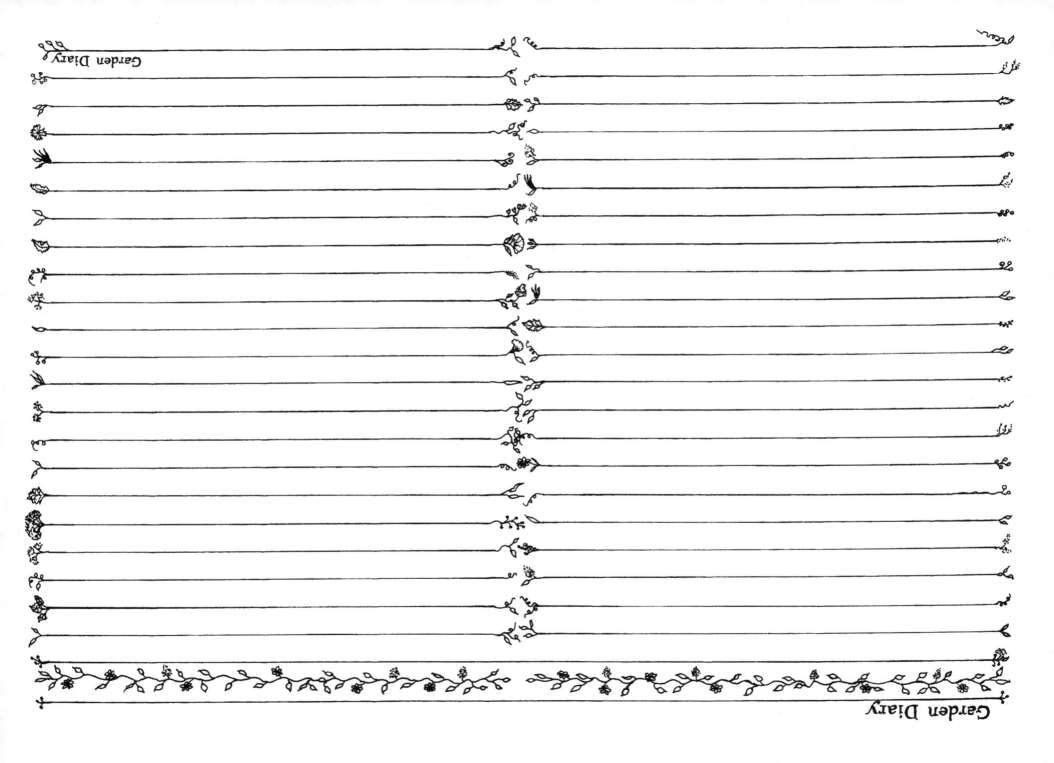

Garden Diary

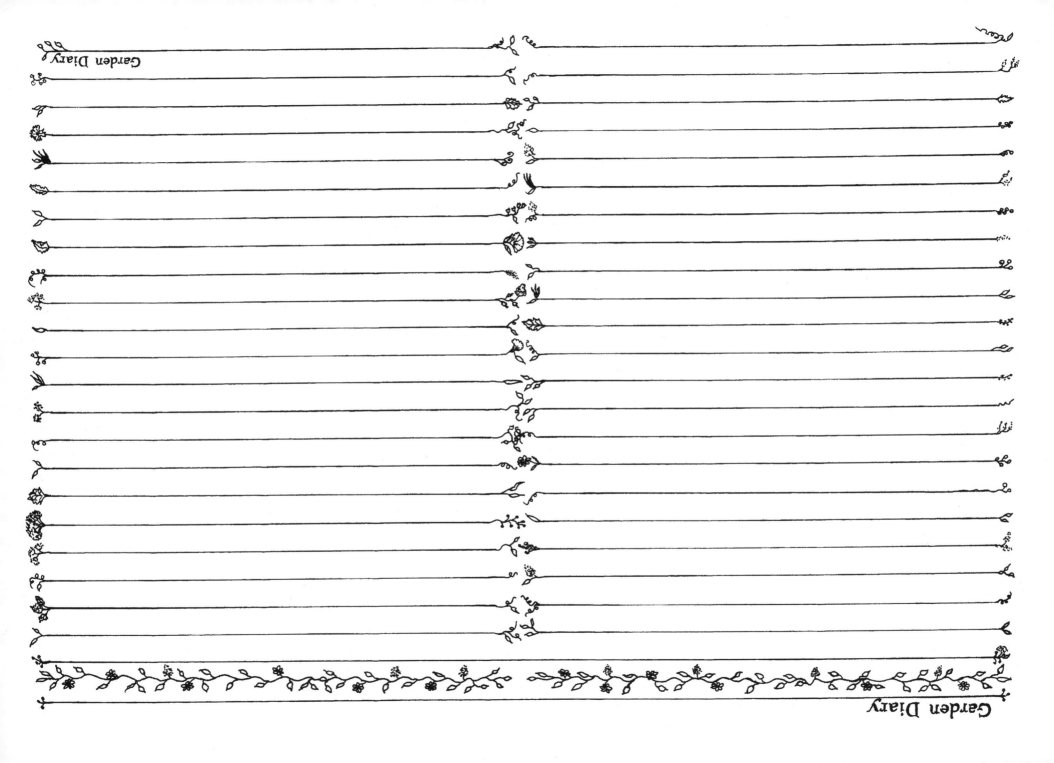

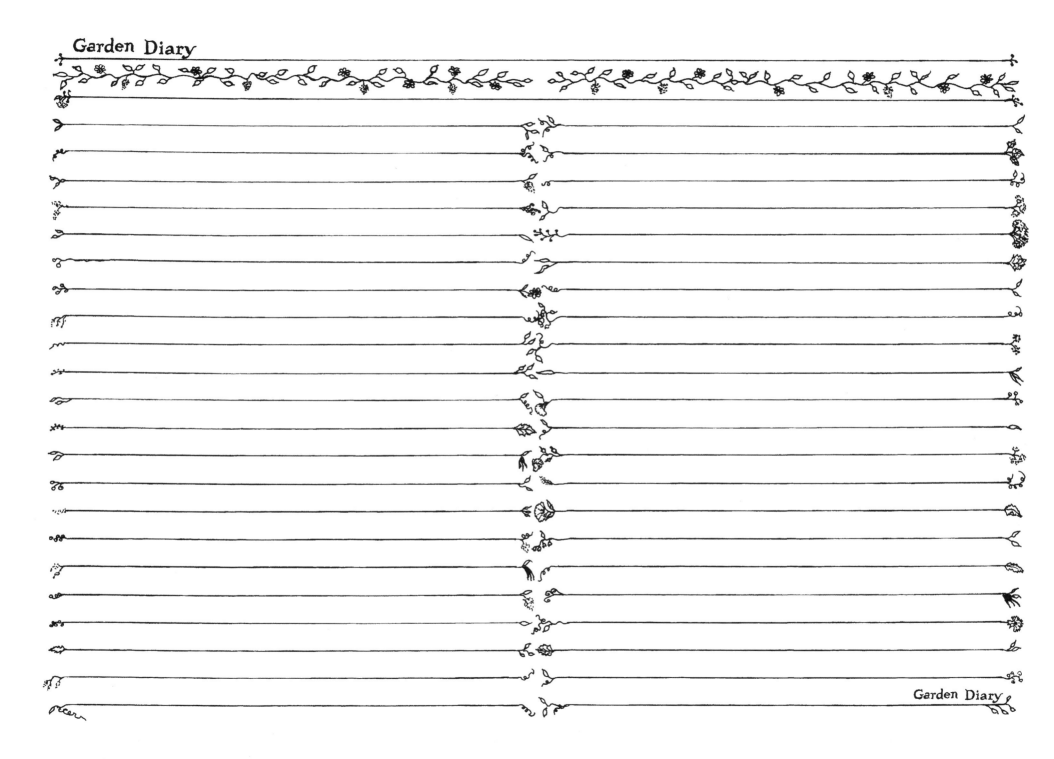

Garden Diary

Garden Diary

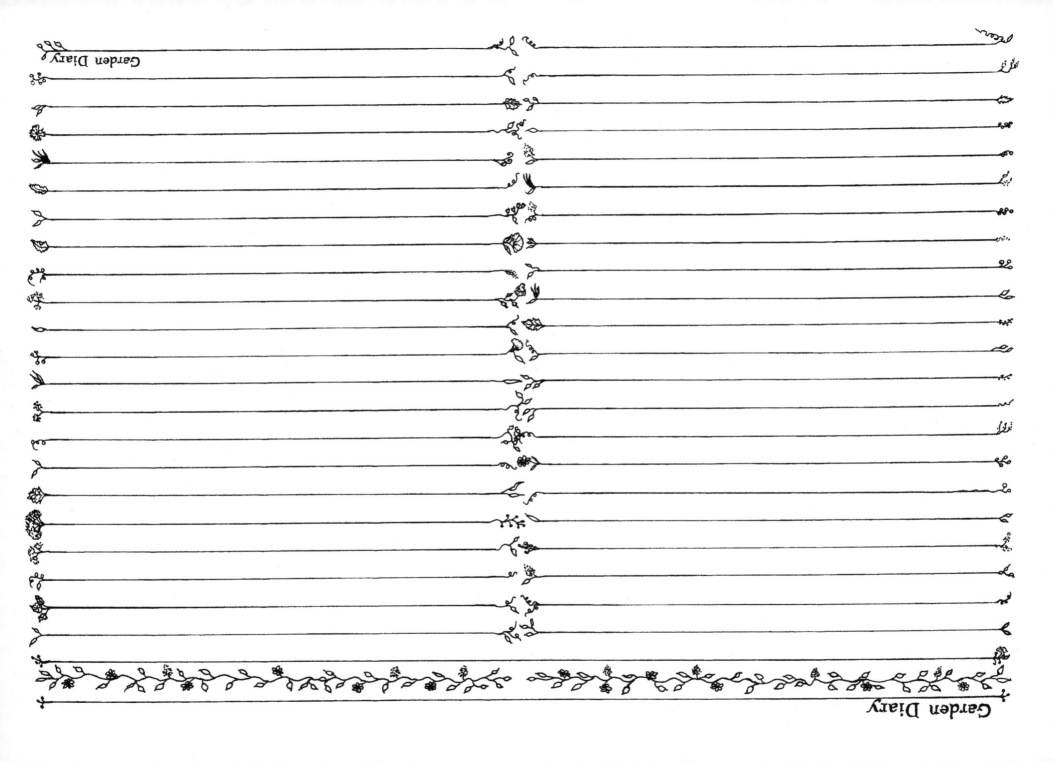

Garden Diary

Garden Diary

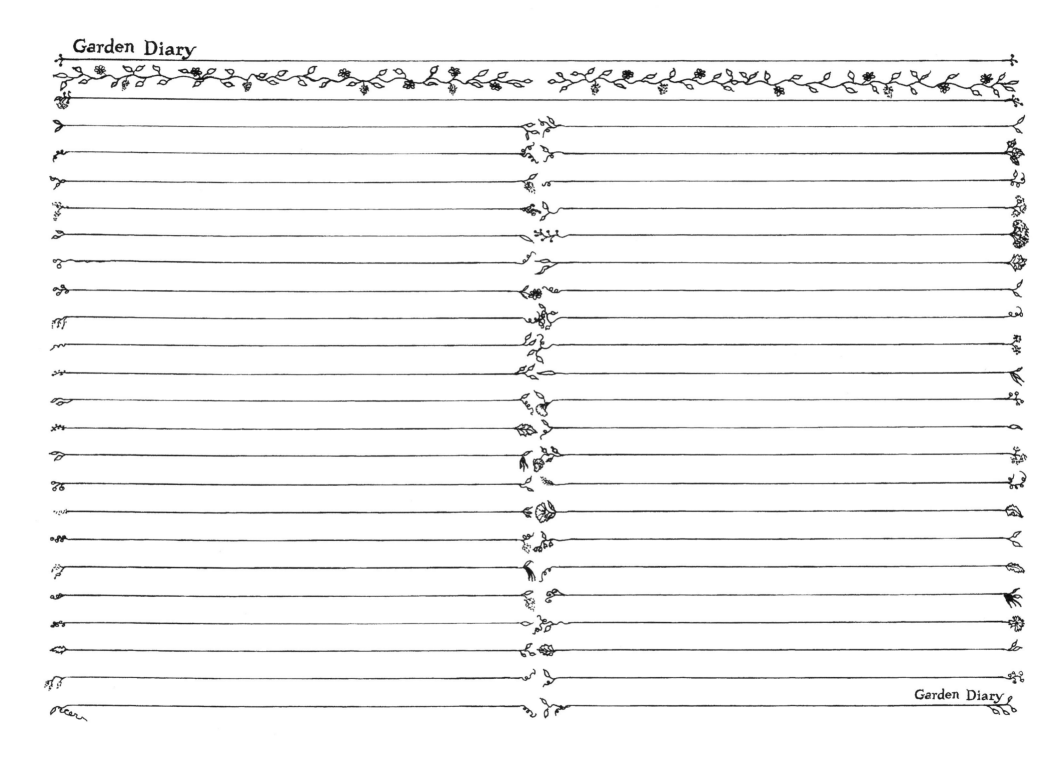

Garden Diary

Garden Diary

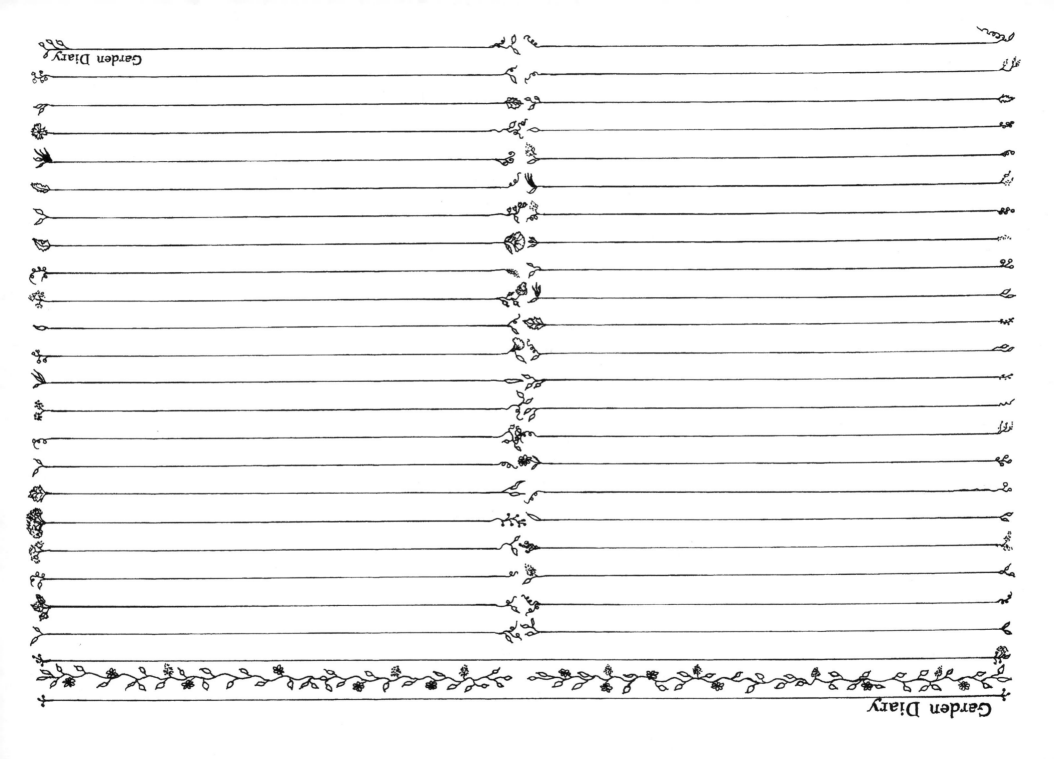

Garden Diary

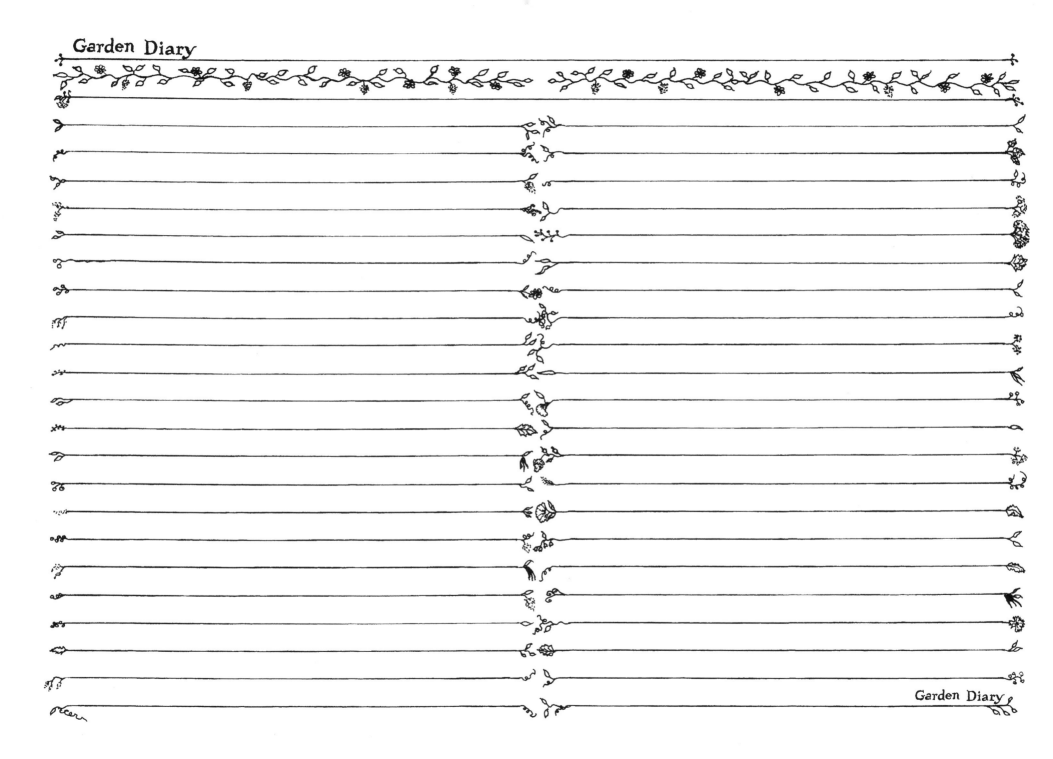

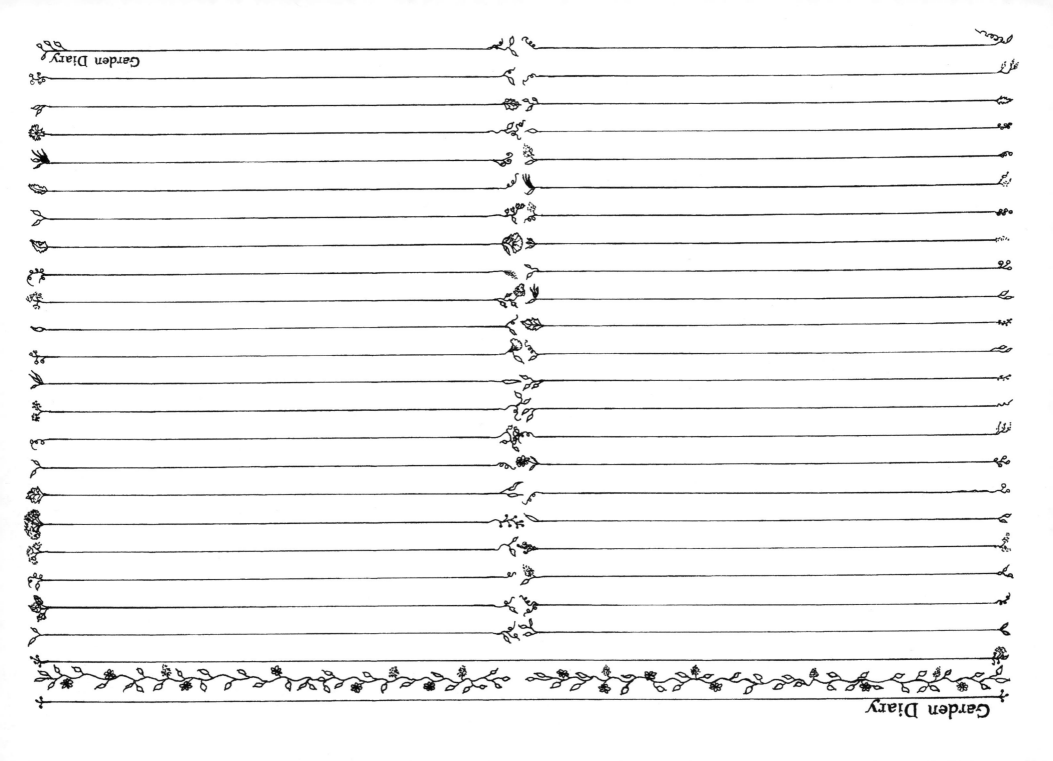

Garden Diary

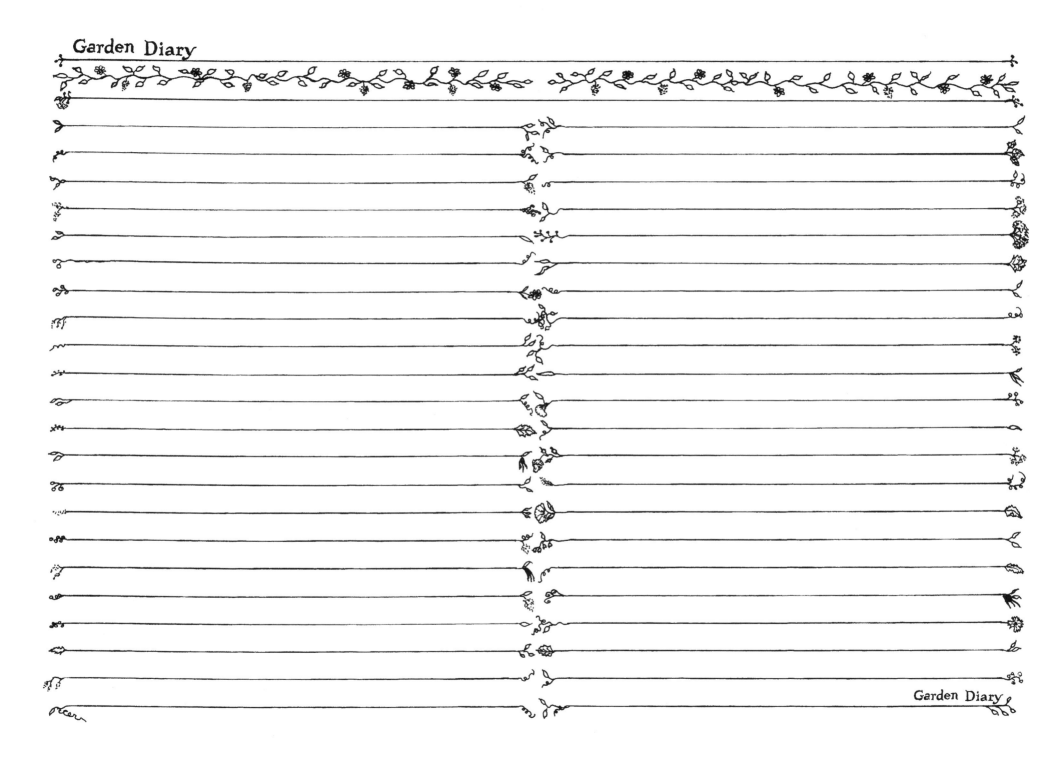

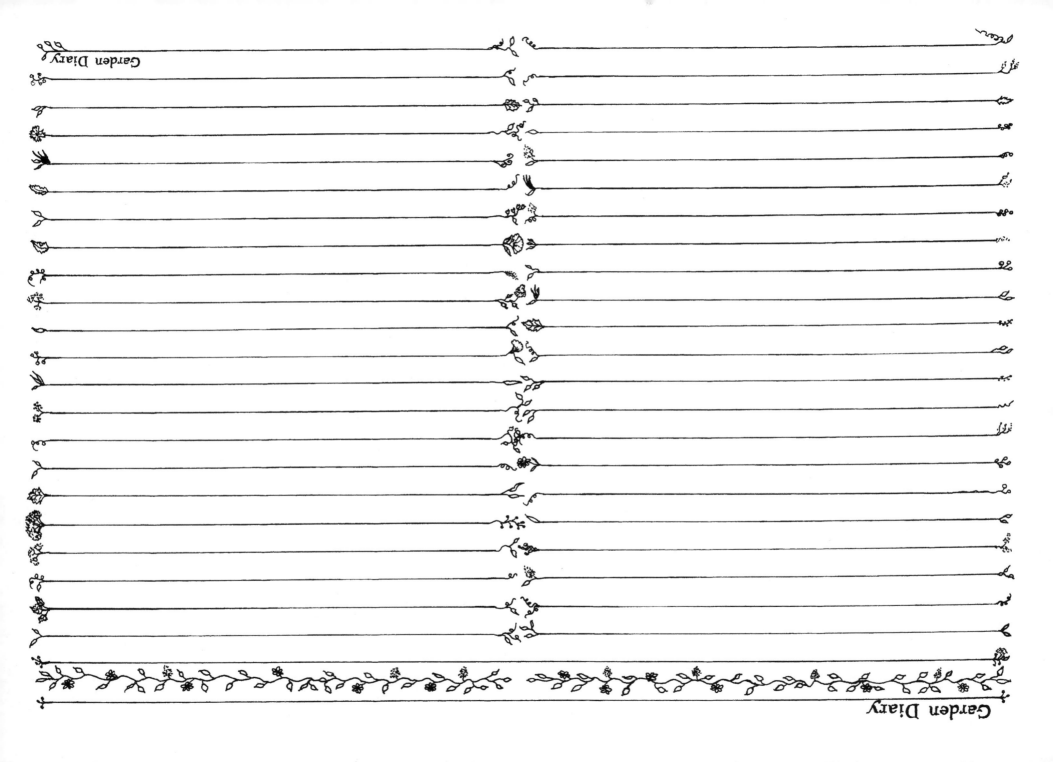

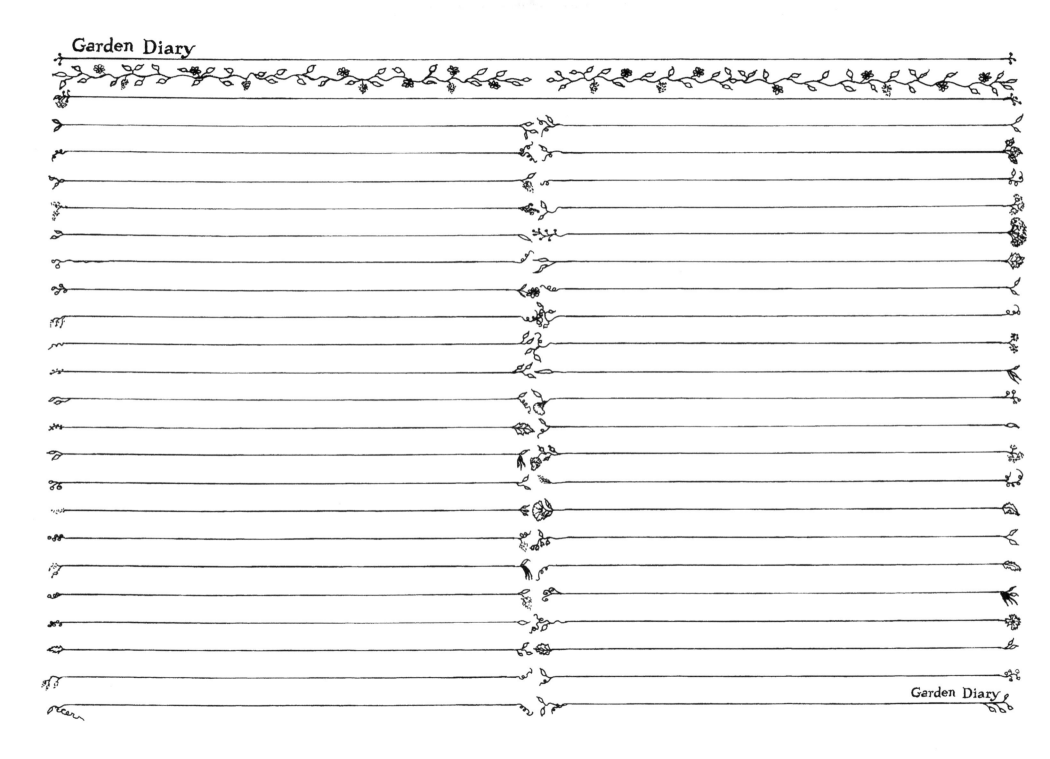

Garden Diary

Garden Diary

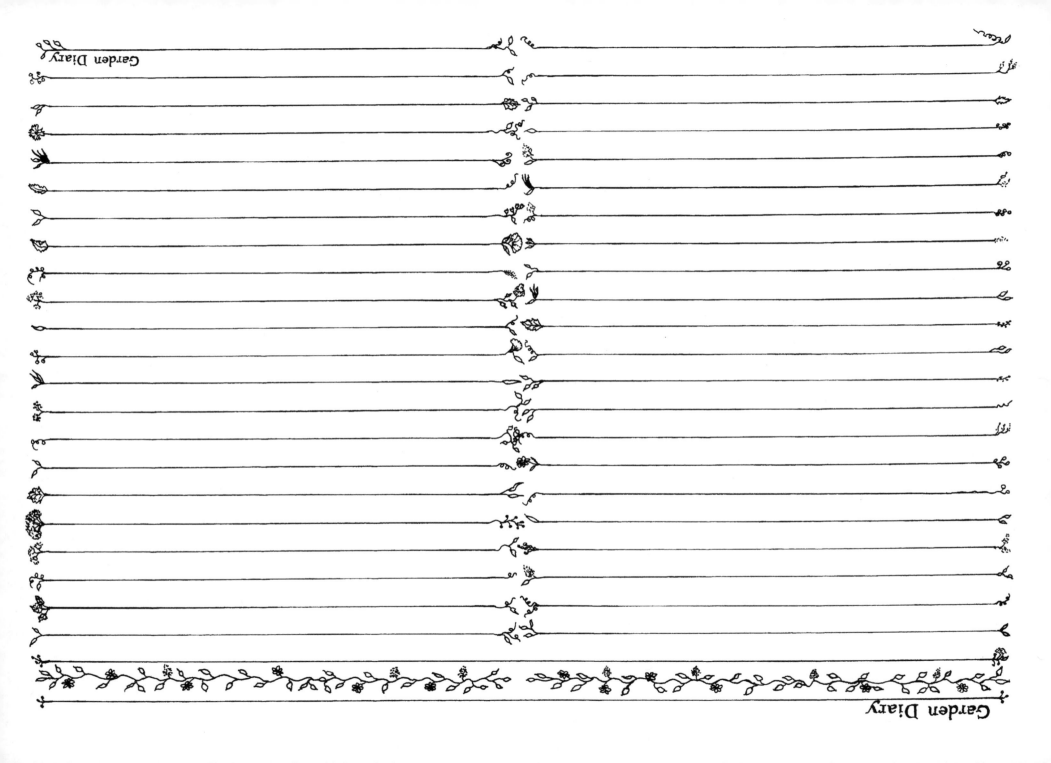

Garden Diary

Garden Diary

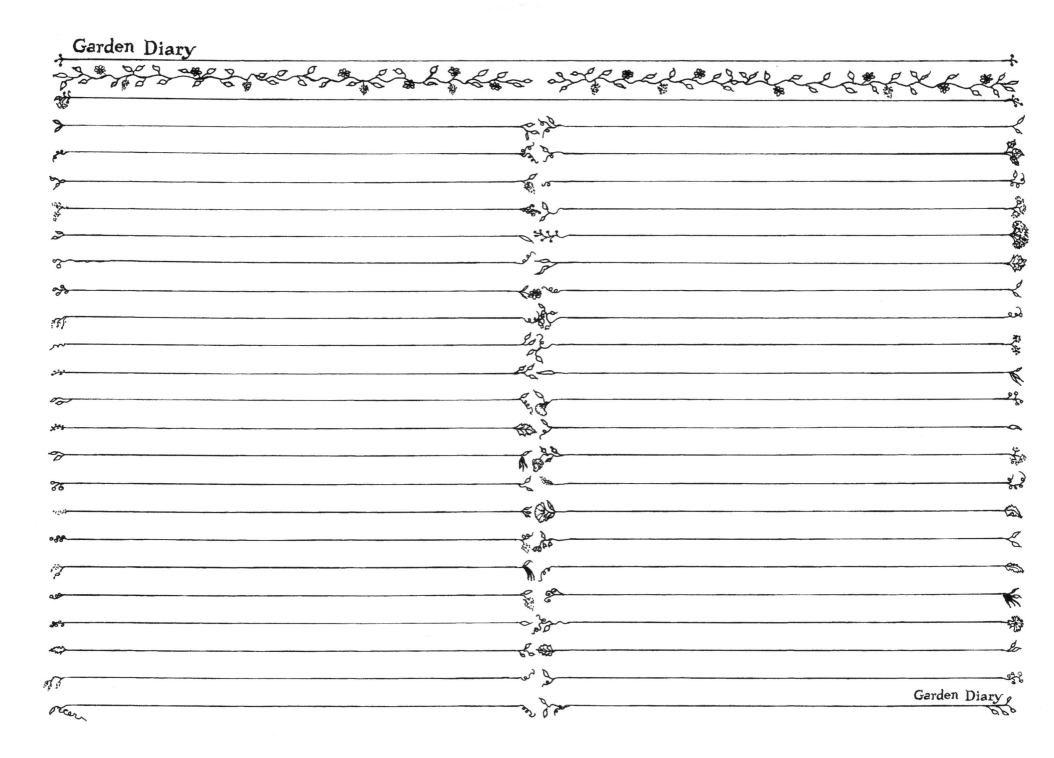

Garden Diary

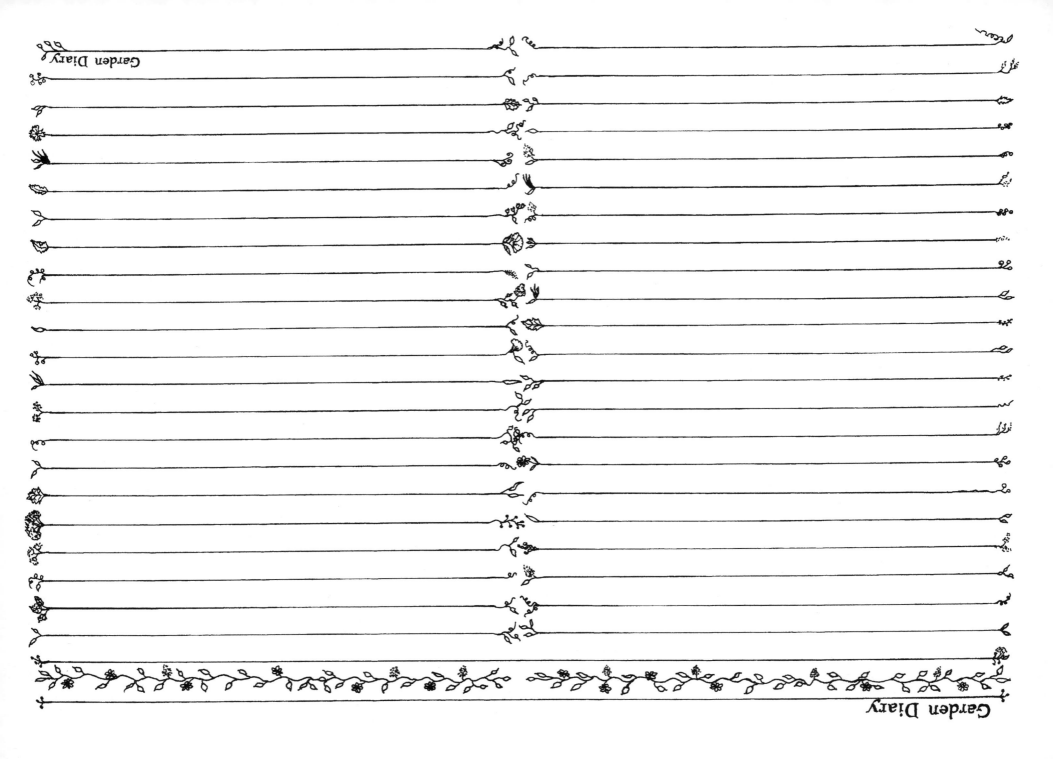

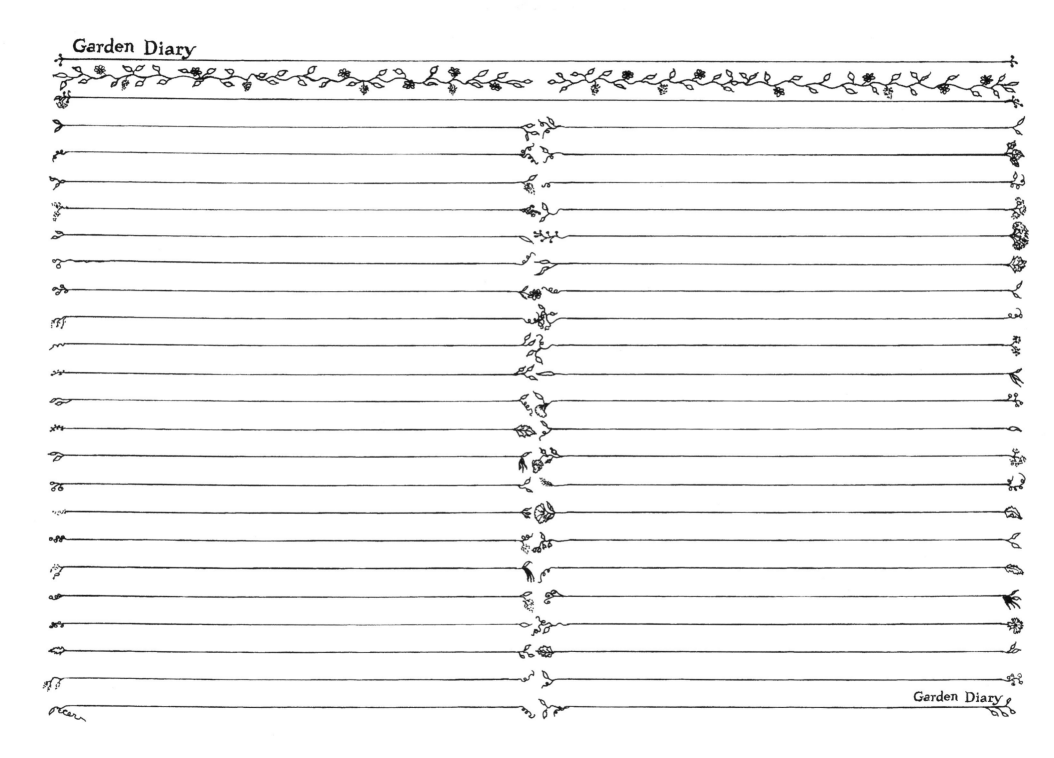

Garden Diary

Garden Diary

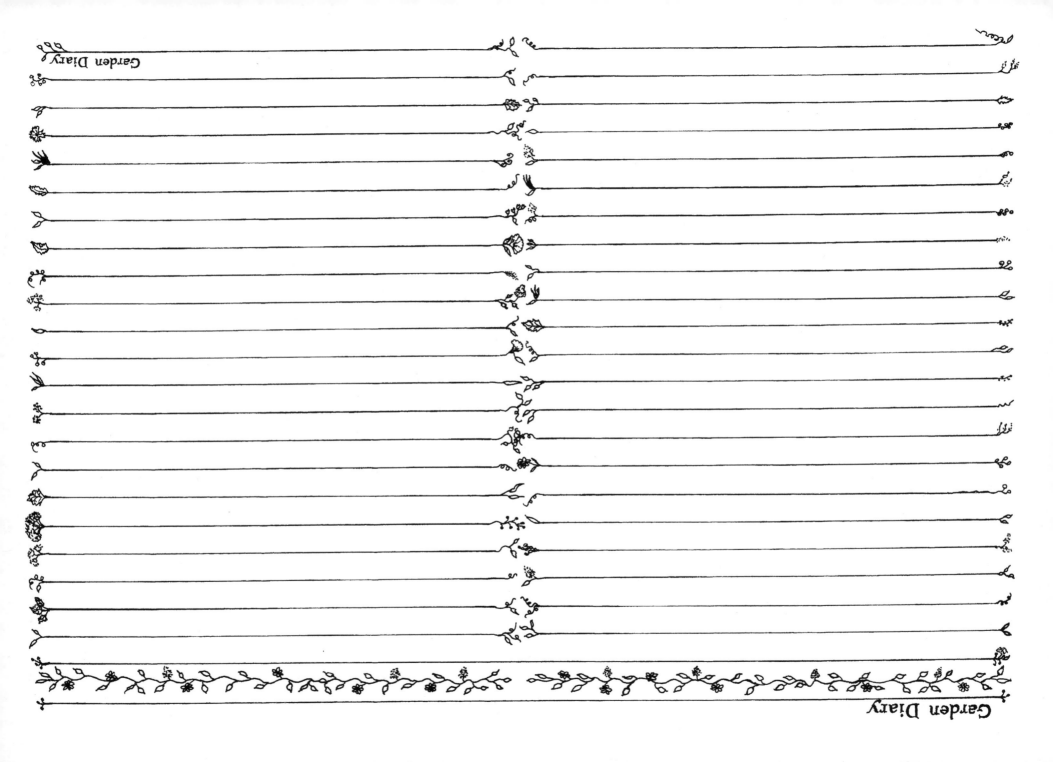

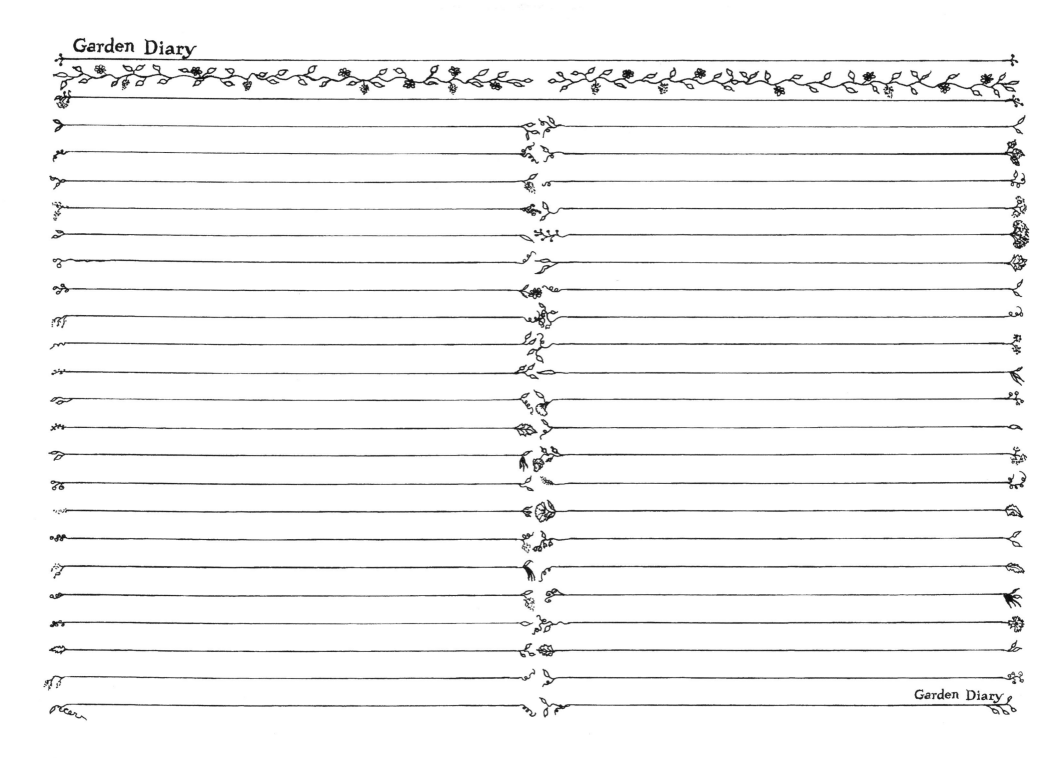

Garden Diary

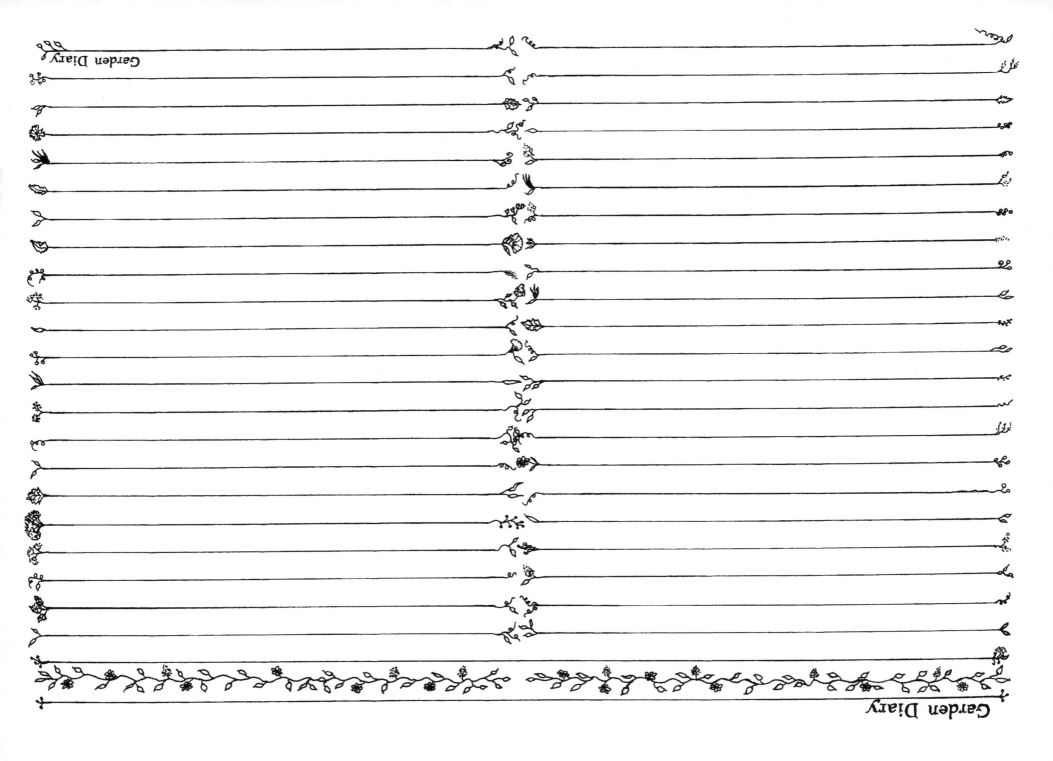

Garden Diary

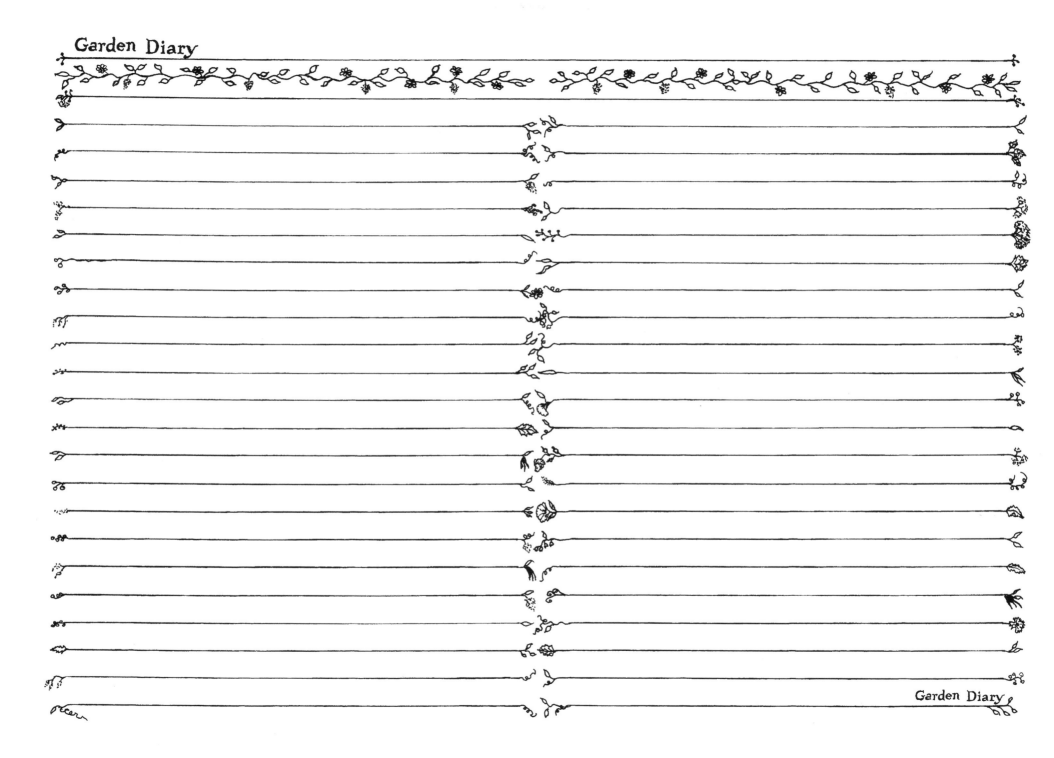

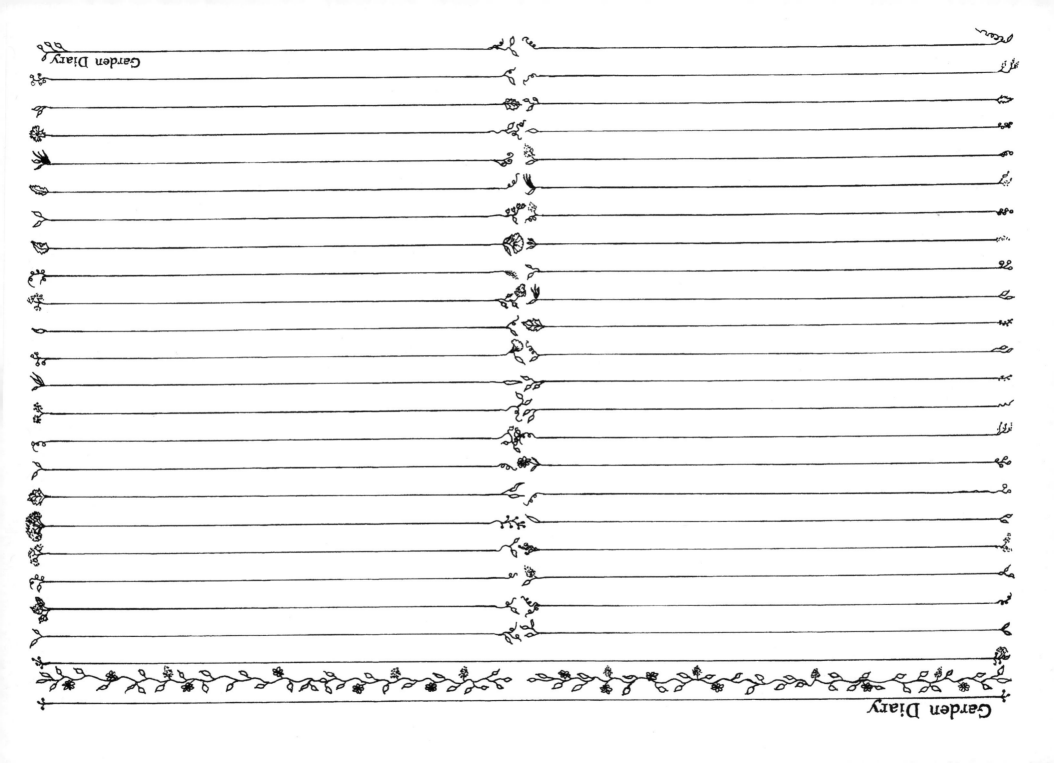

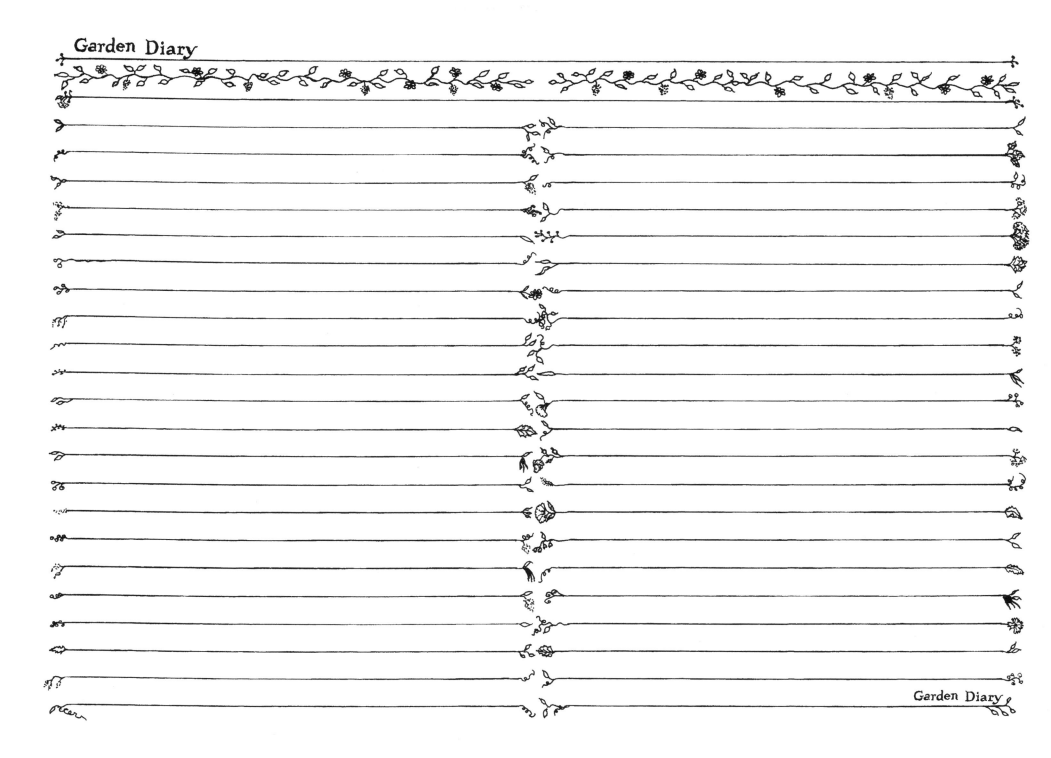

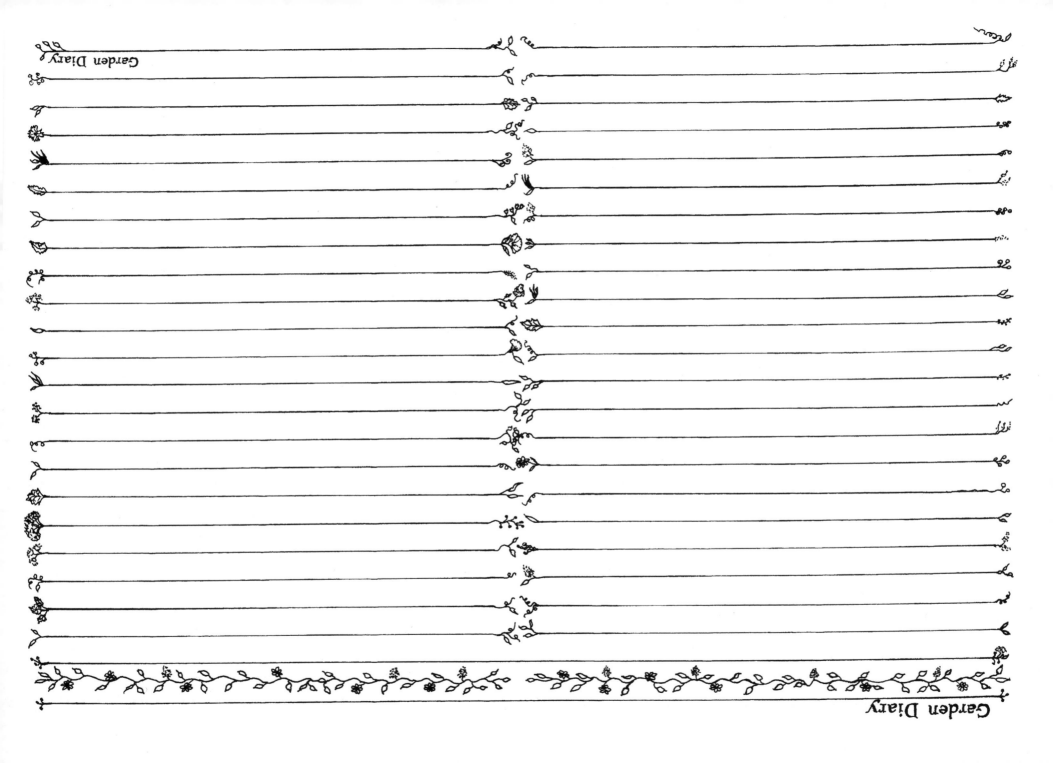

Garden Diary

Garden Diary

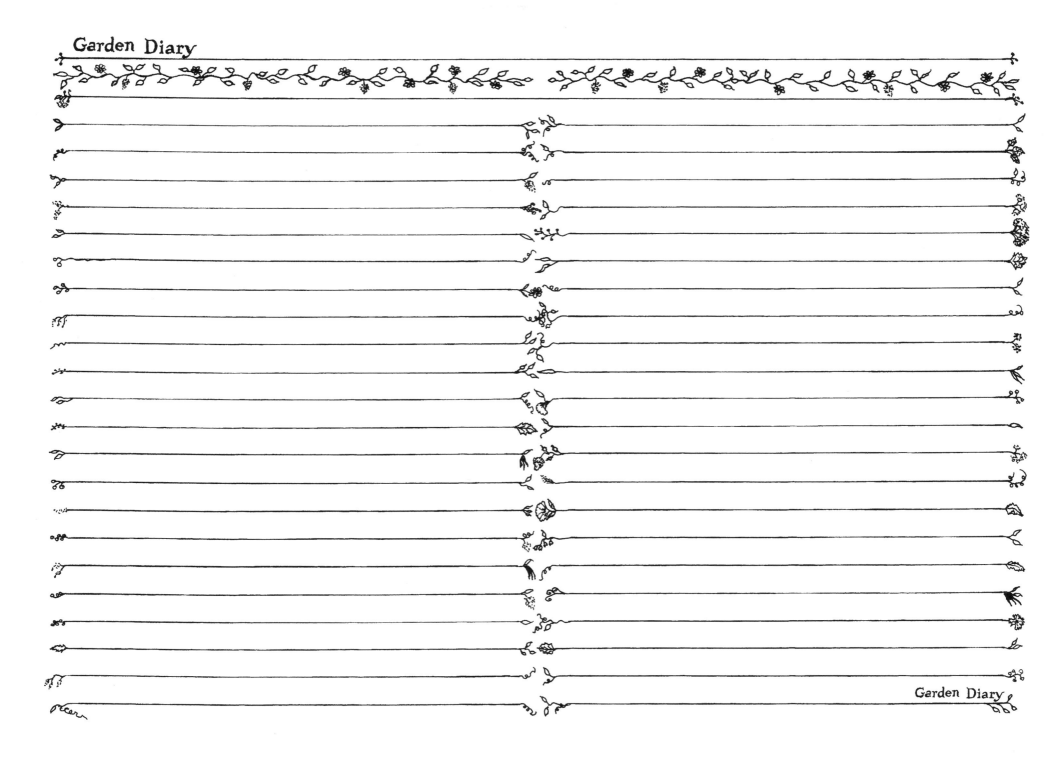

Garden Diary

Garden Diary

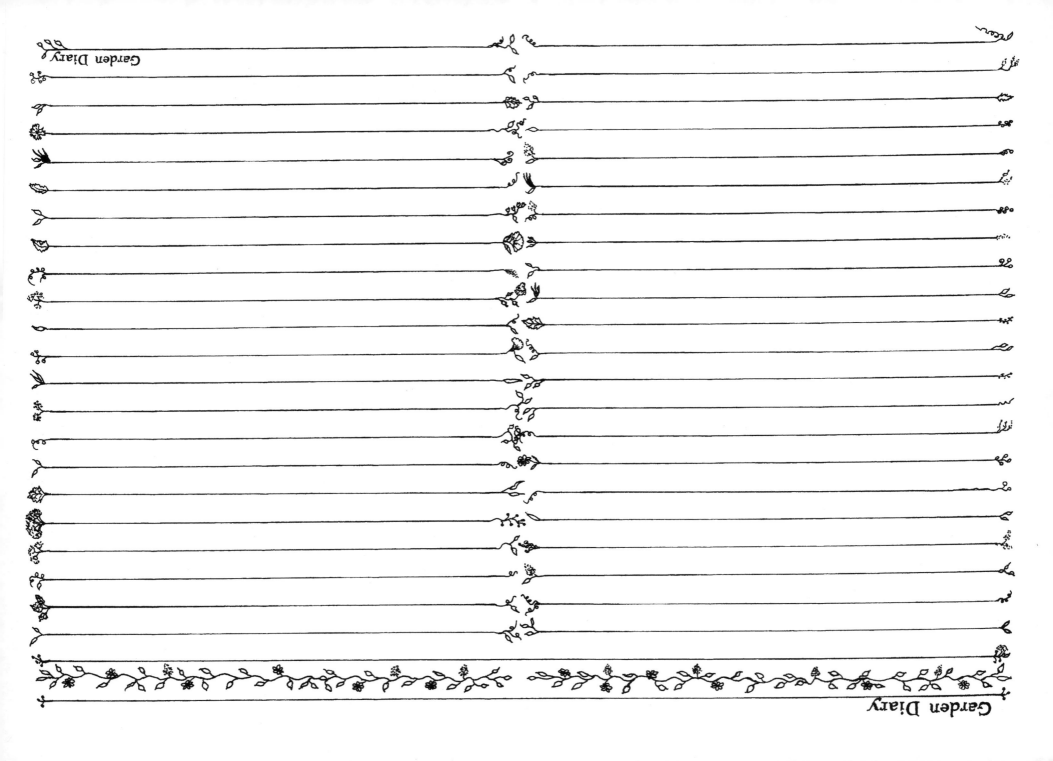

Garden Diary

Garden Diary

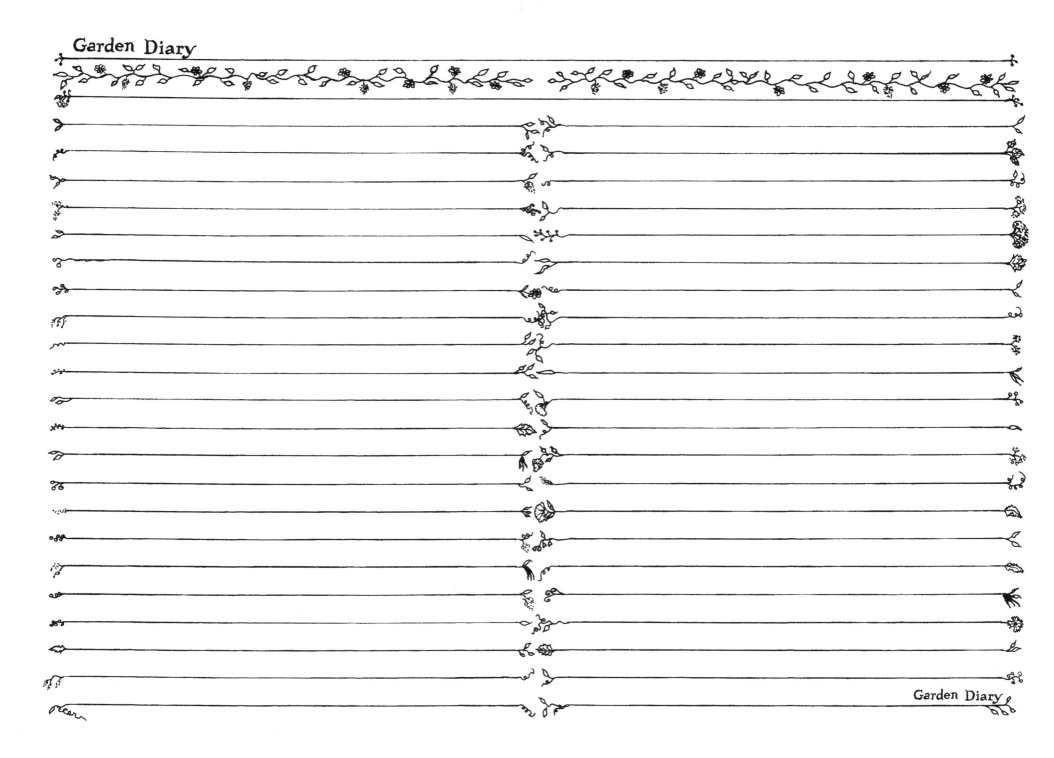

Garden Diary

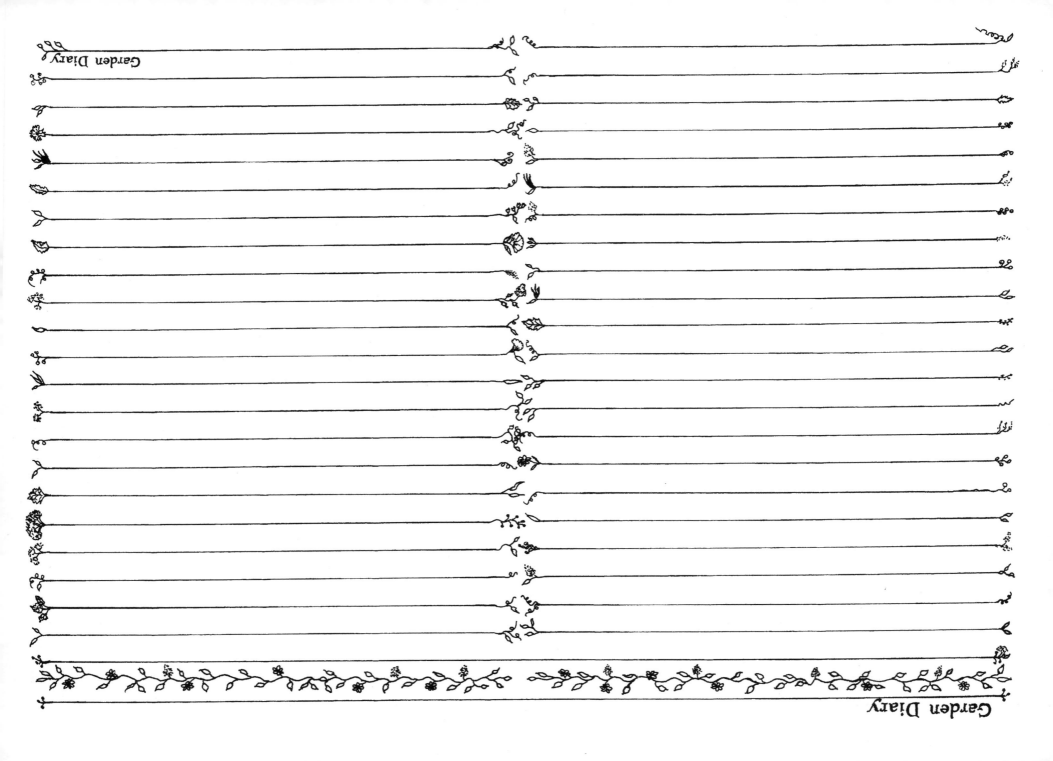

Garden Diary

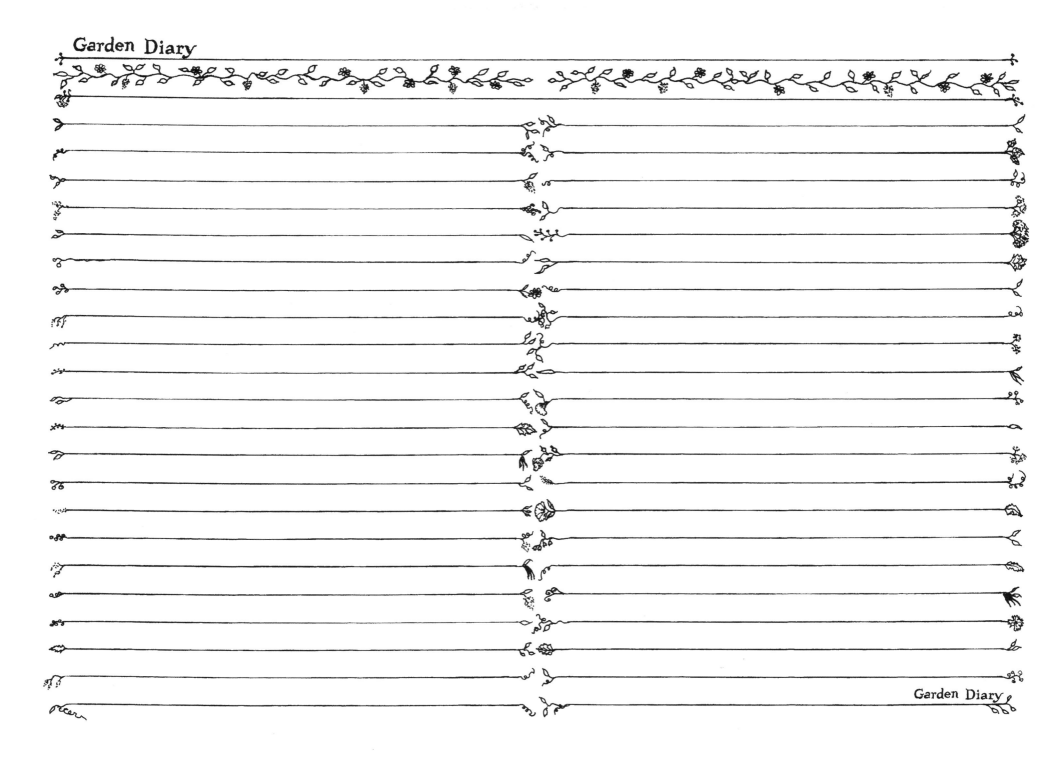

Garden Diary

Garden Diary

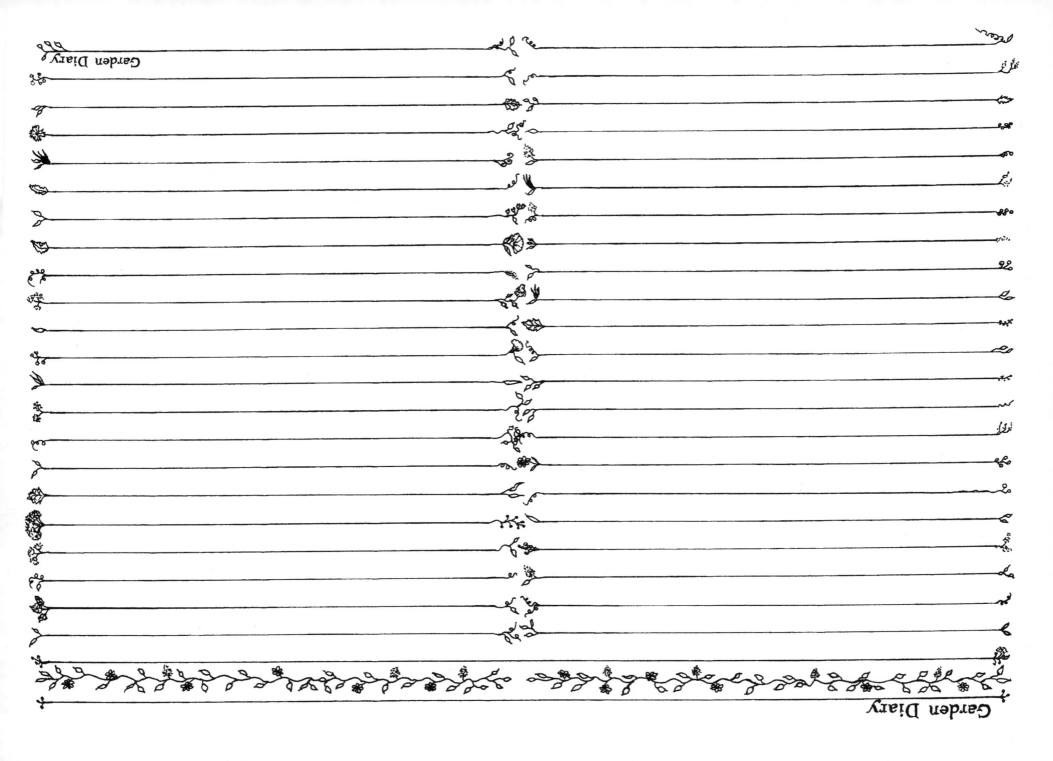

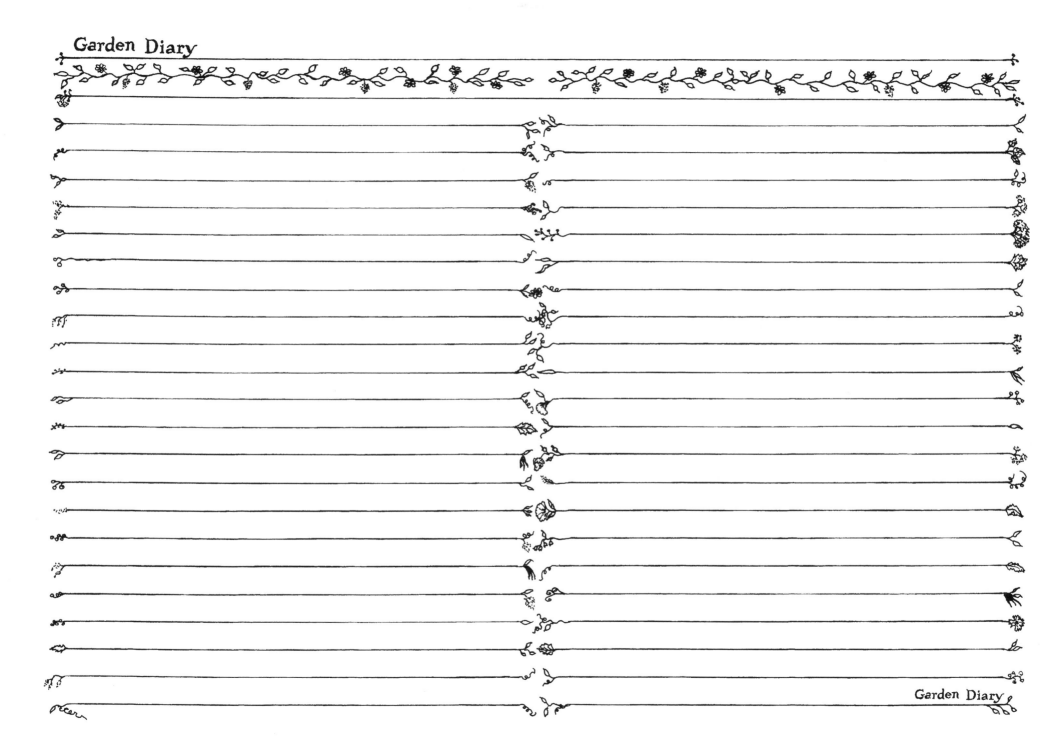

Garden Diary

Garden Diary

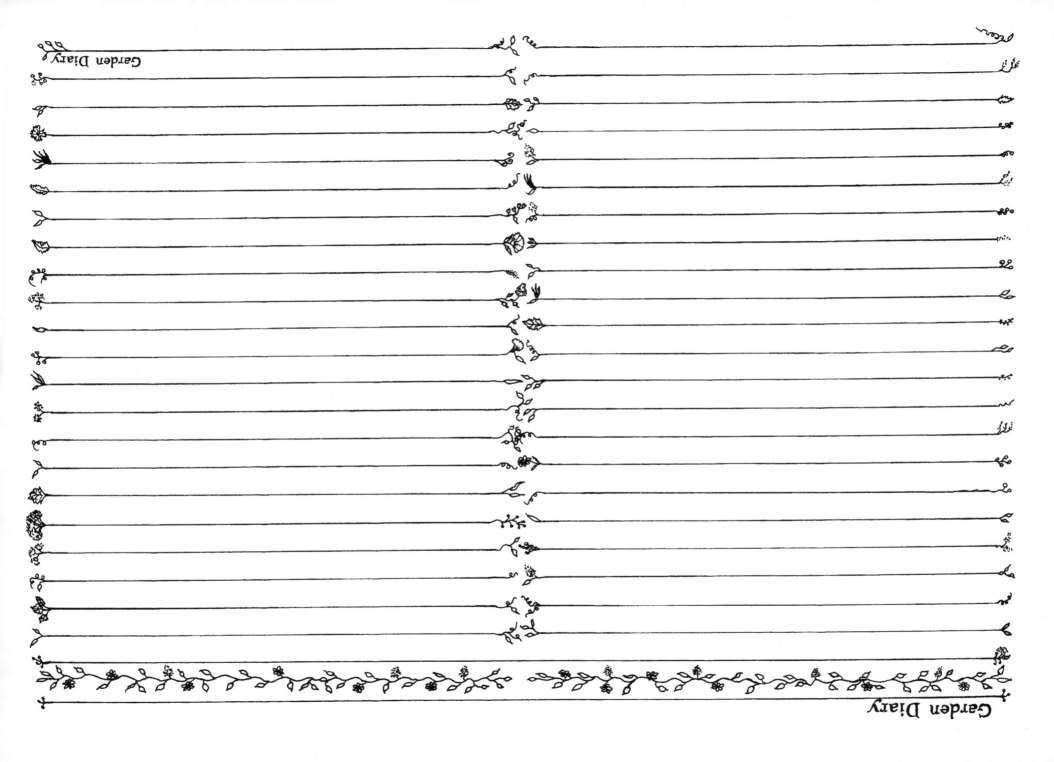

Garden Diary

Garden Diary

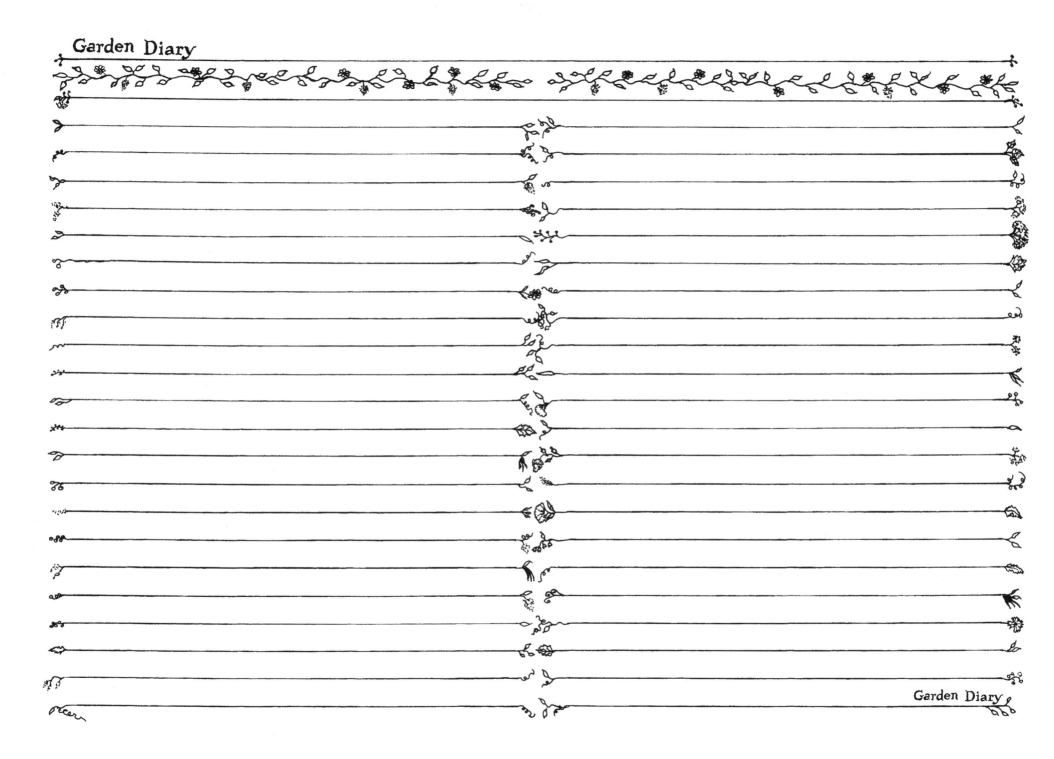

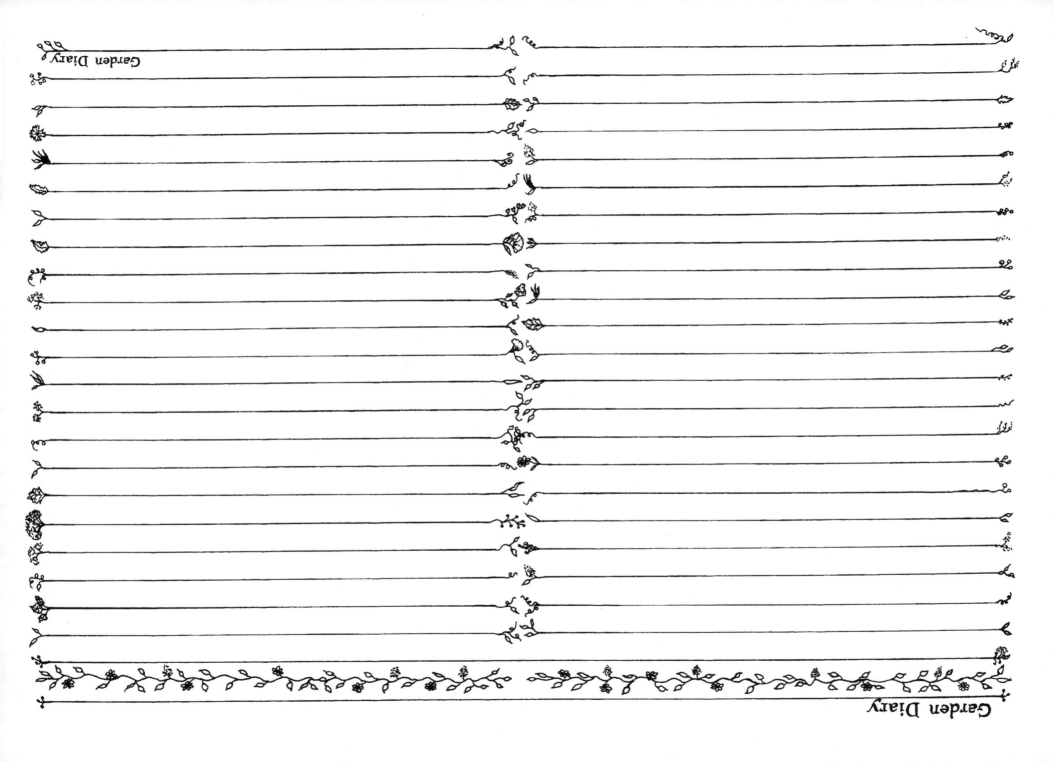

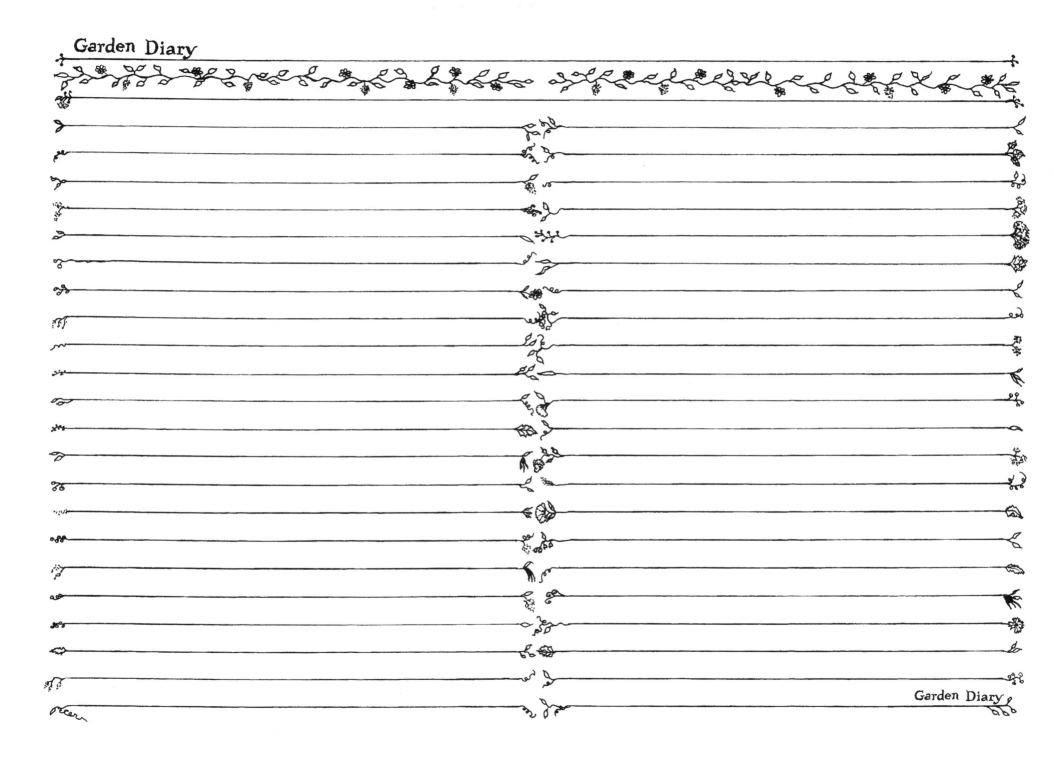

Garden Diary

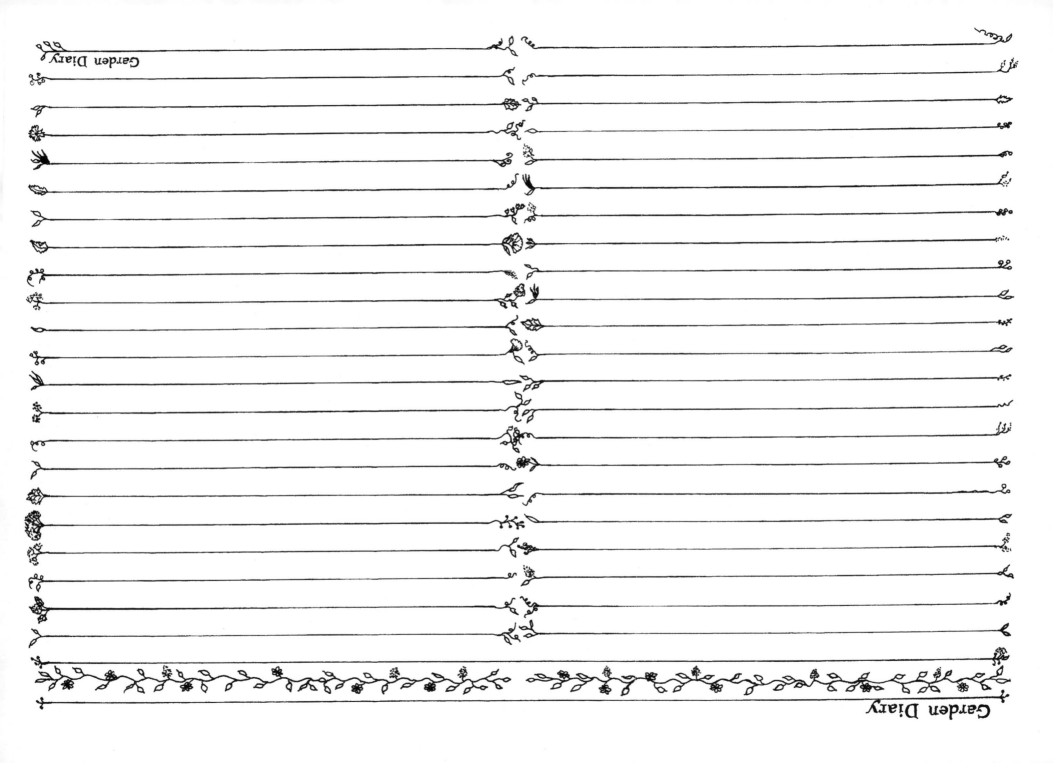

Garden Diary

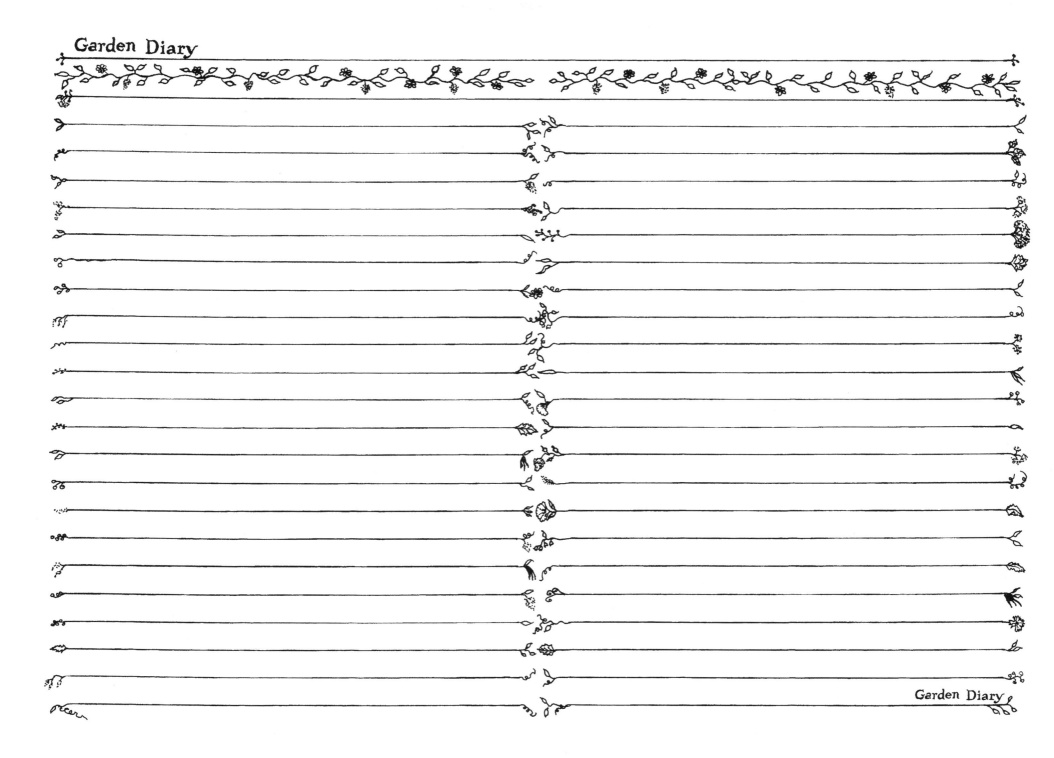

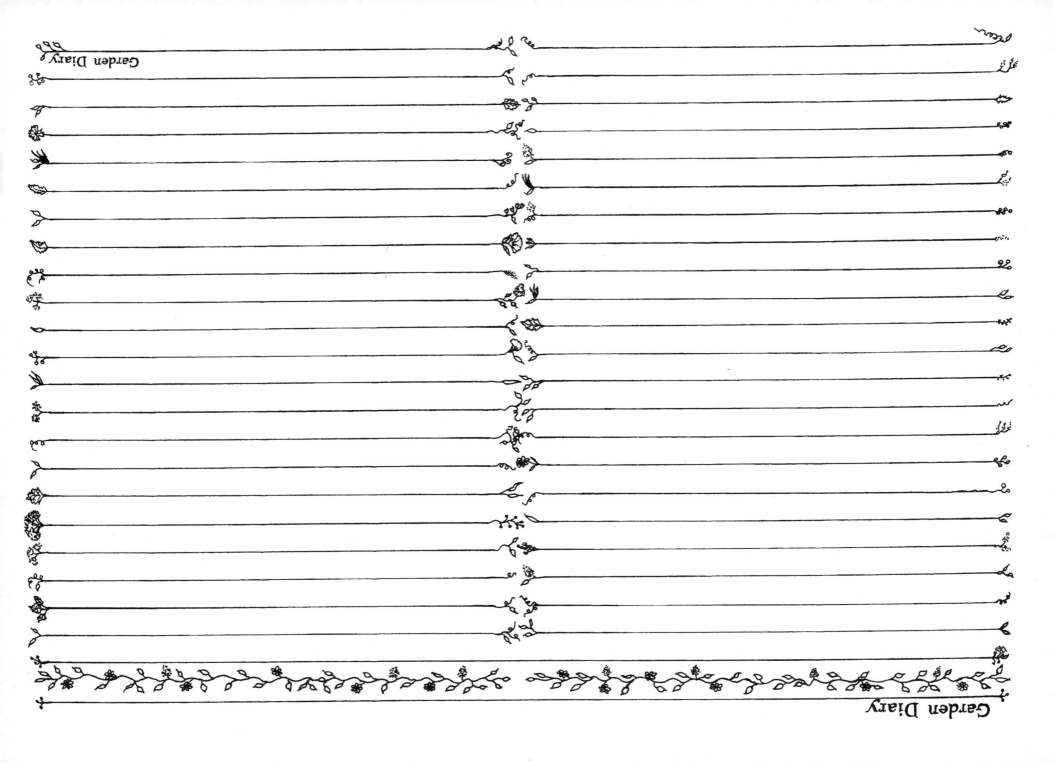

Garden Diary

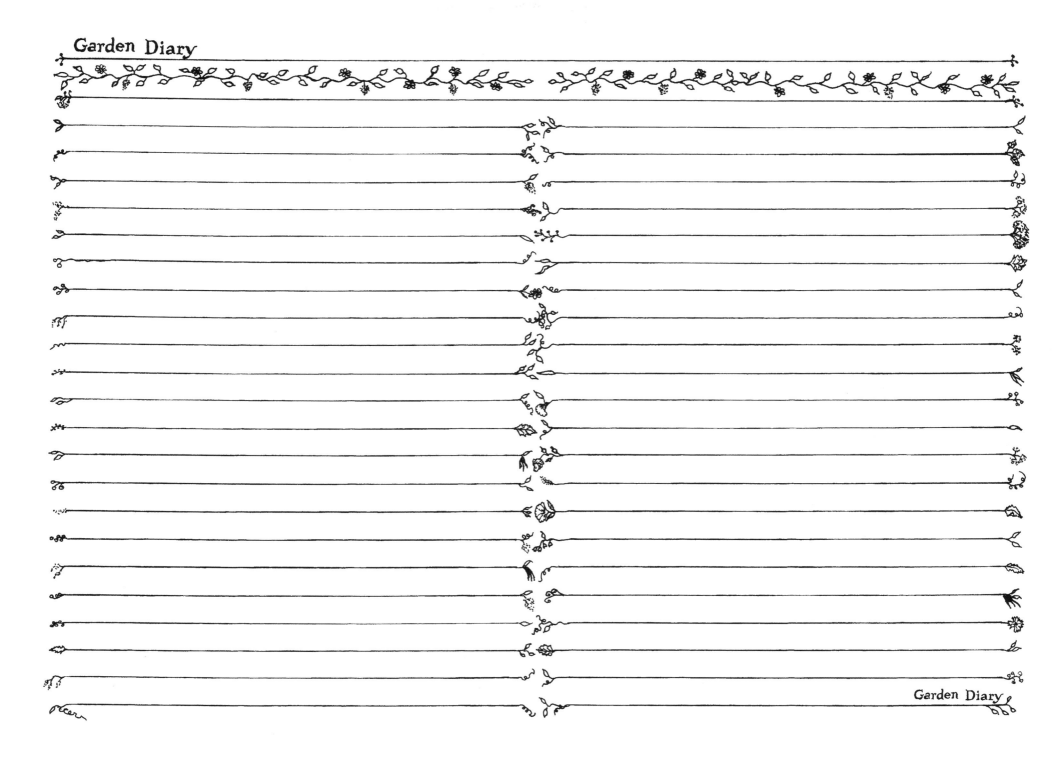

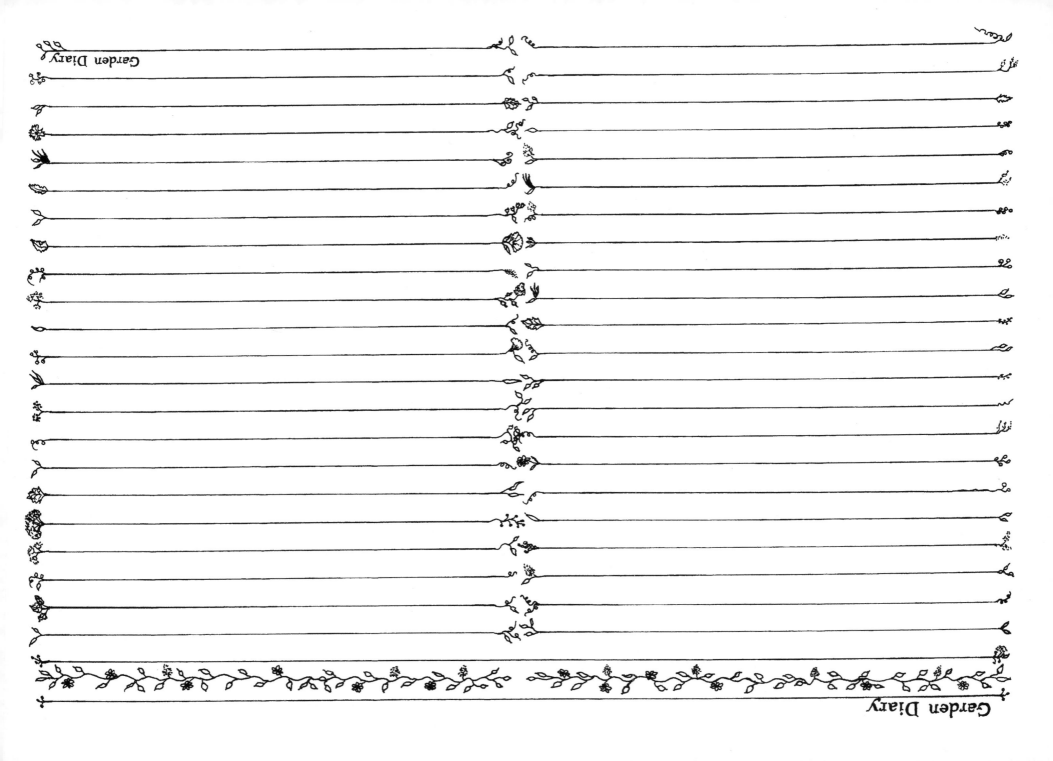

Garden Diary

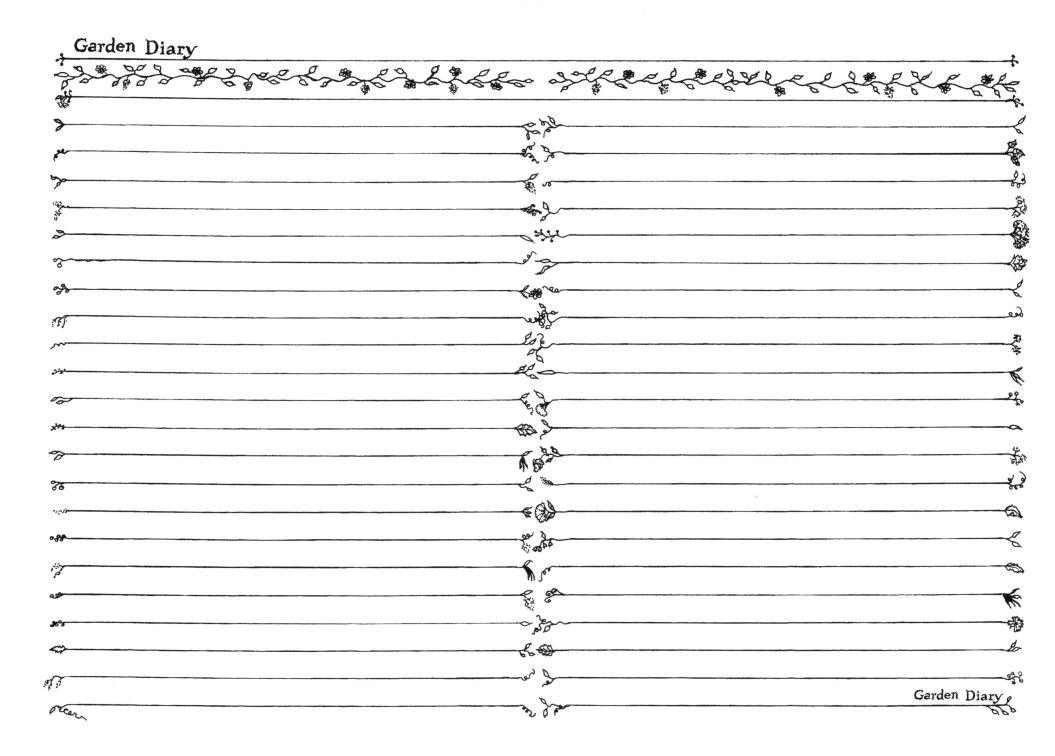

Garden Diary

Garden Diary

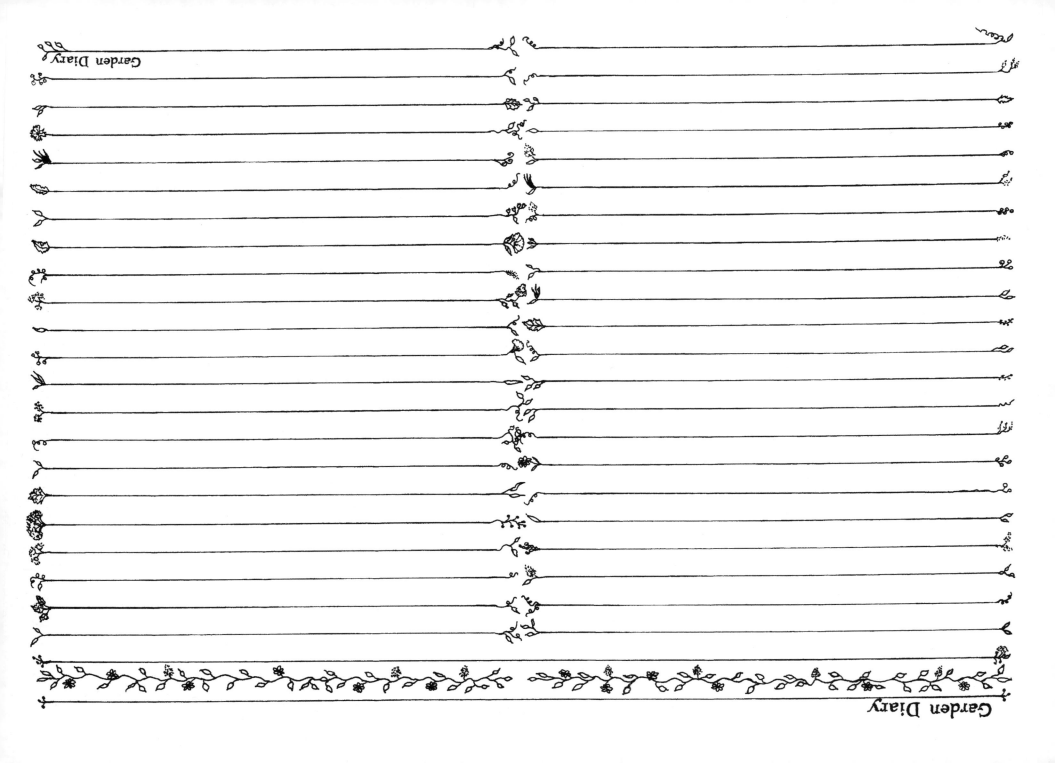

Garden Diary

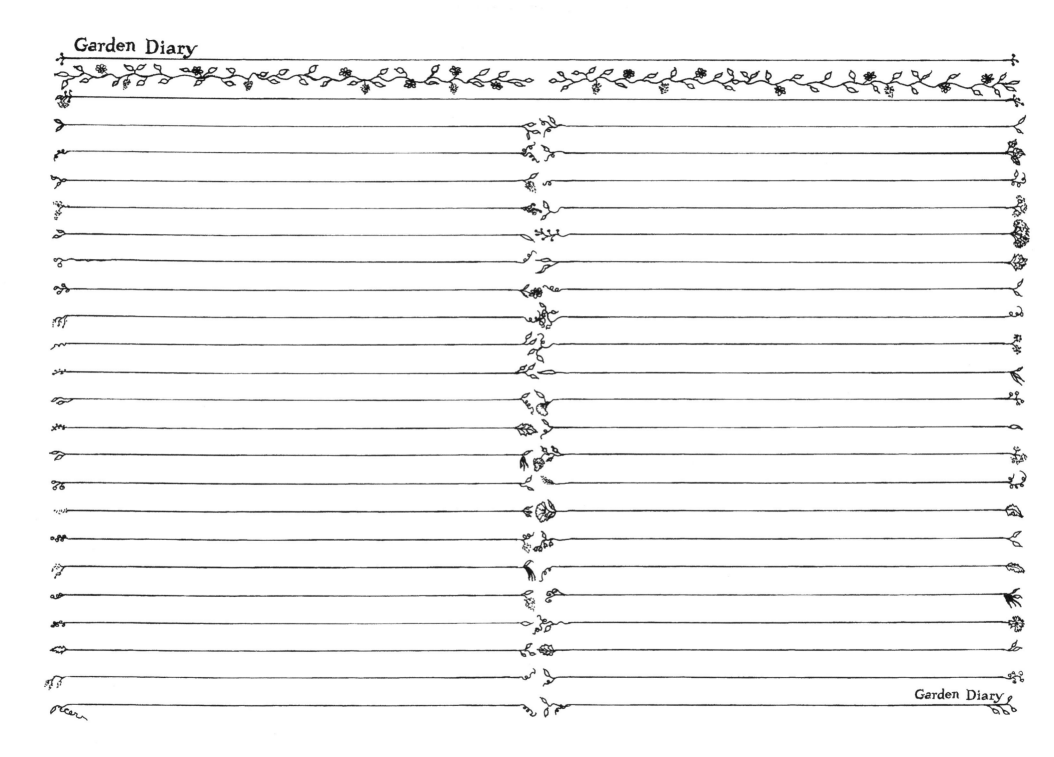

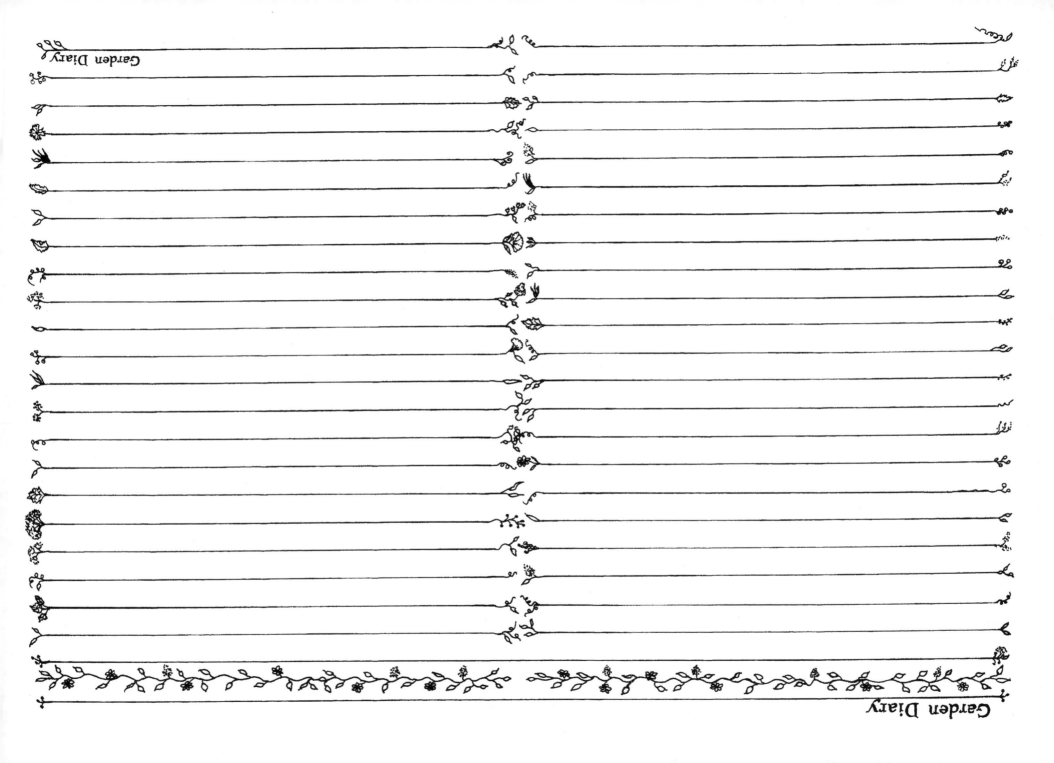

Garden Diary

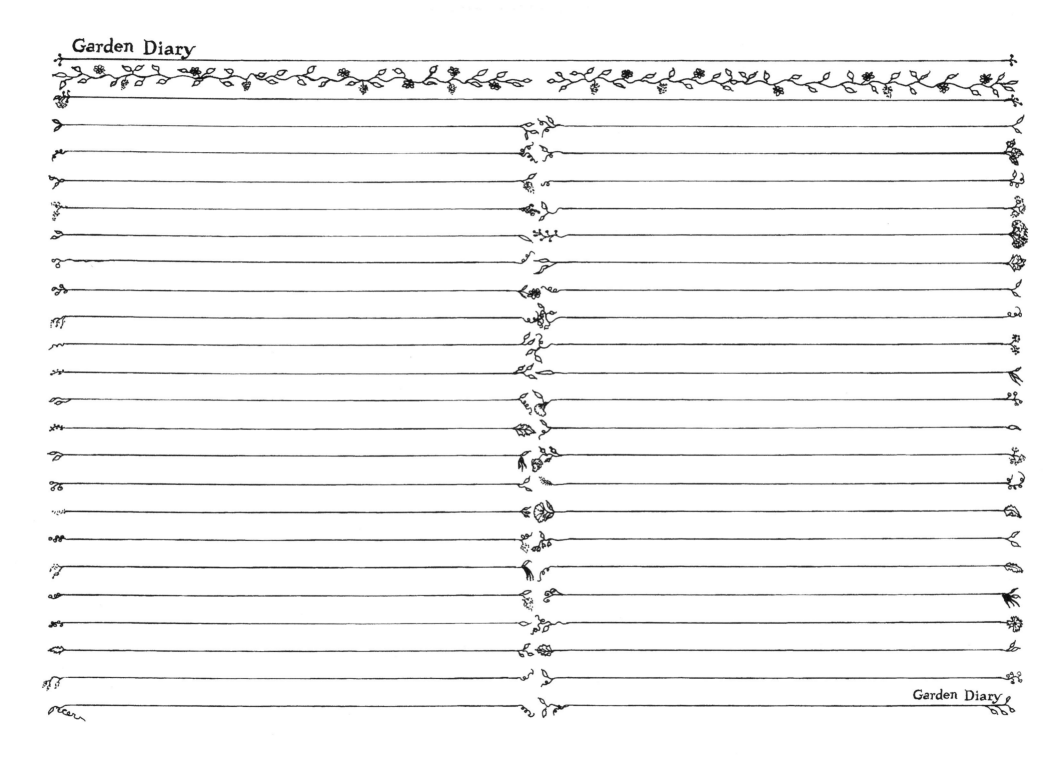

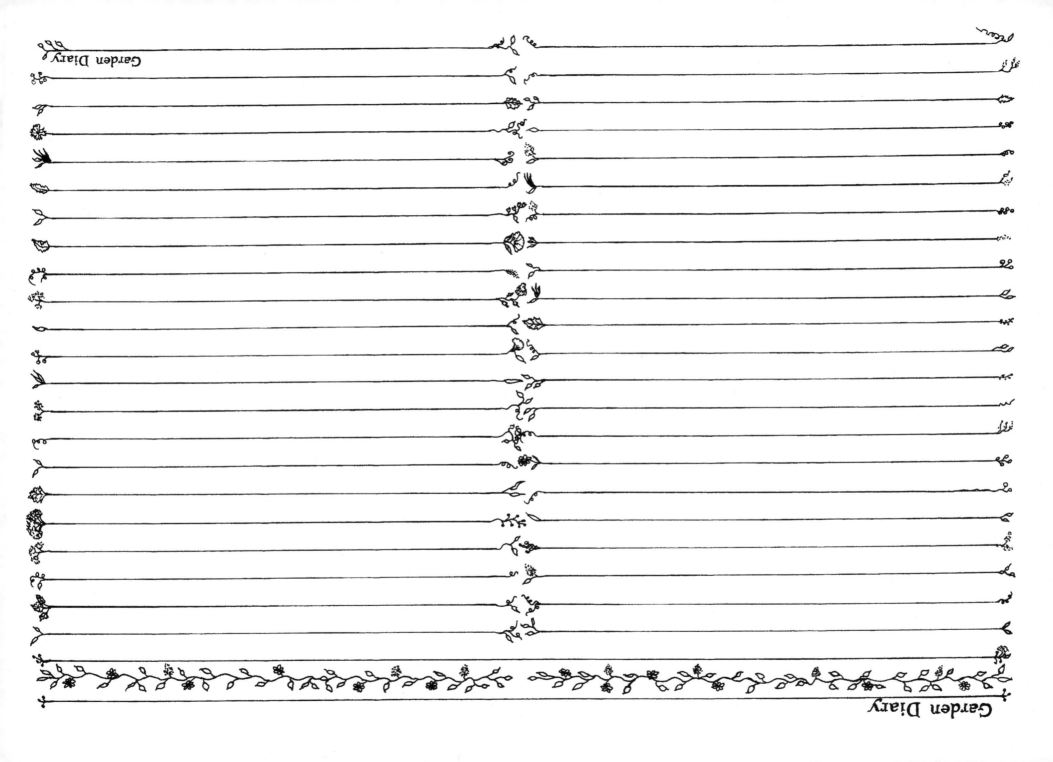

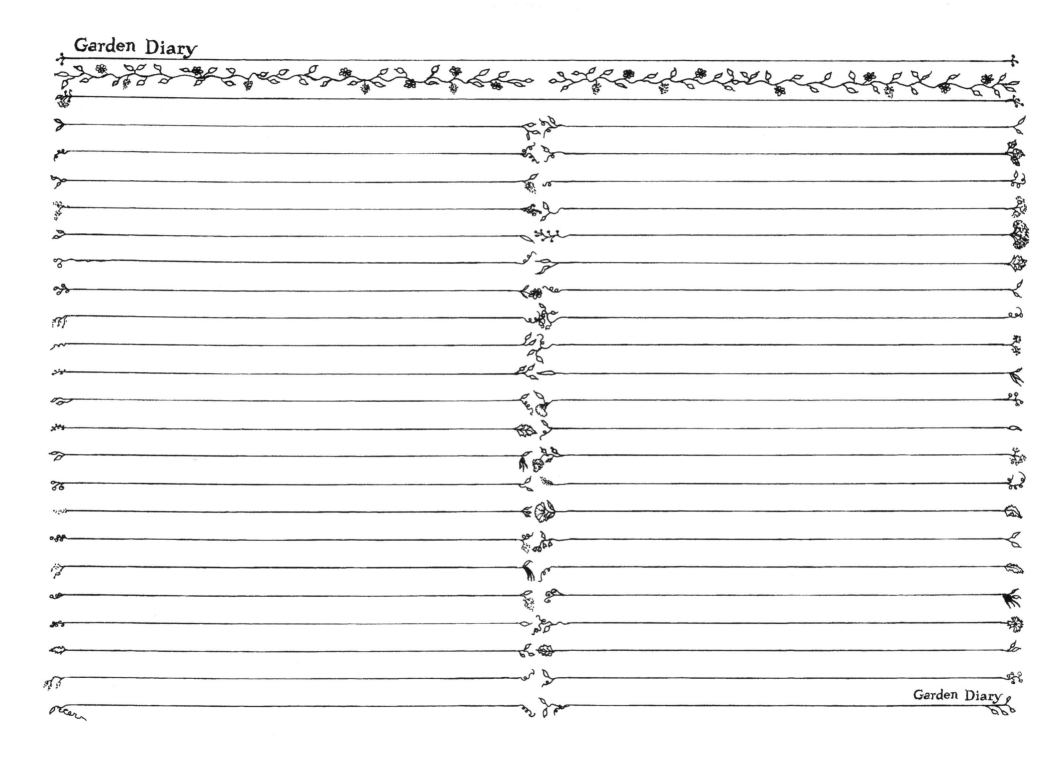

Garden Diary

Garden Diary

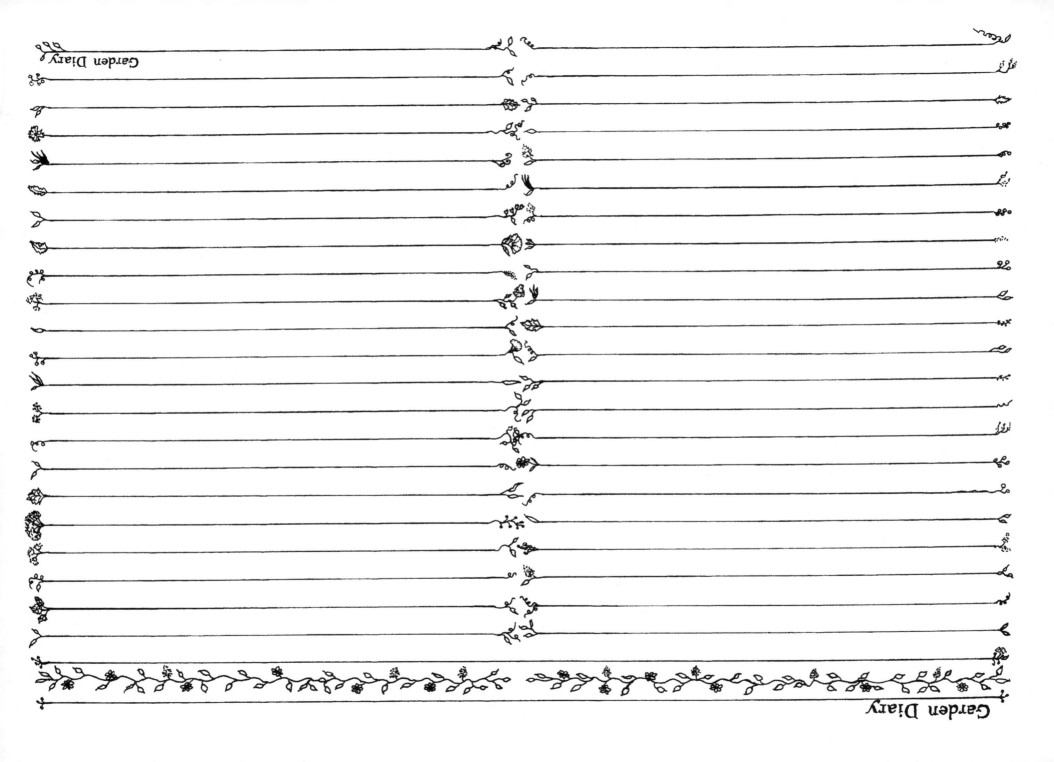

Garden Diary

Garden Diary

Garden Diary

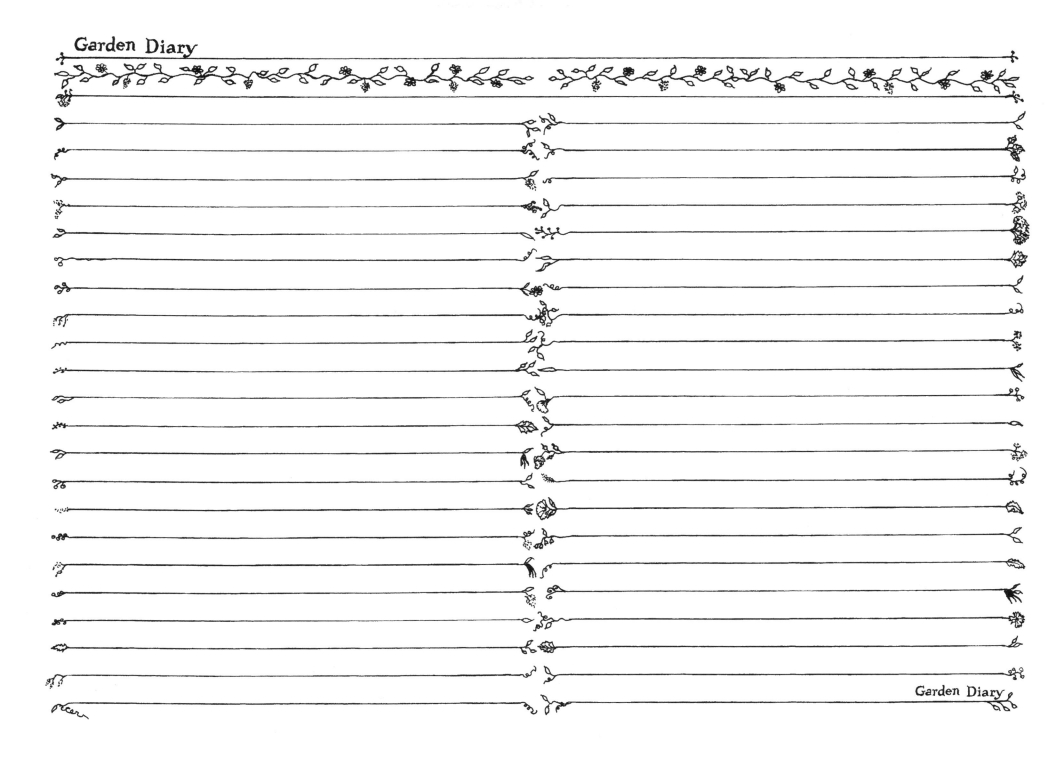

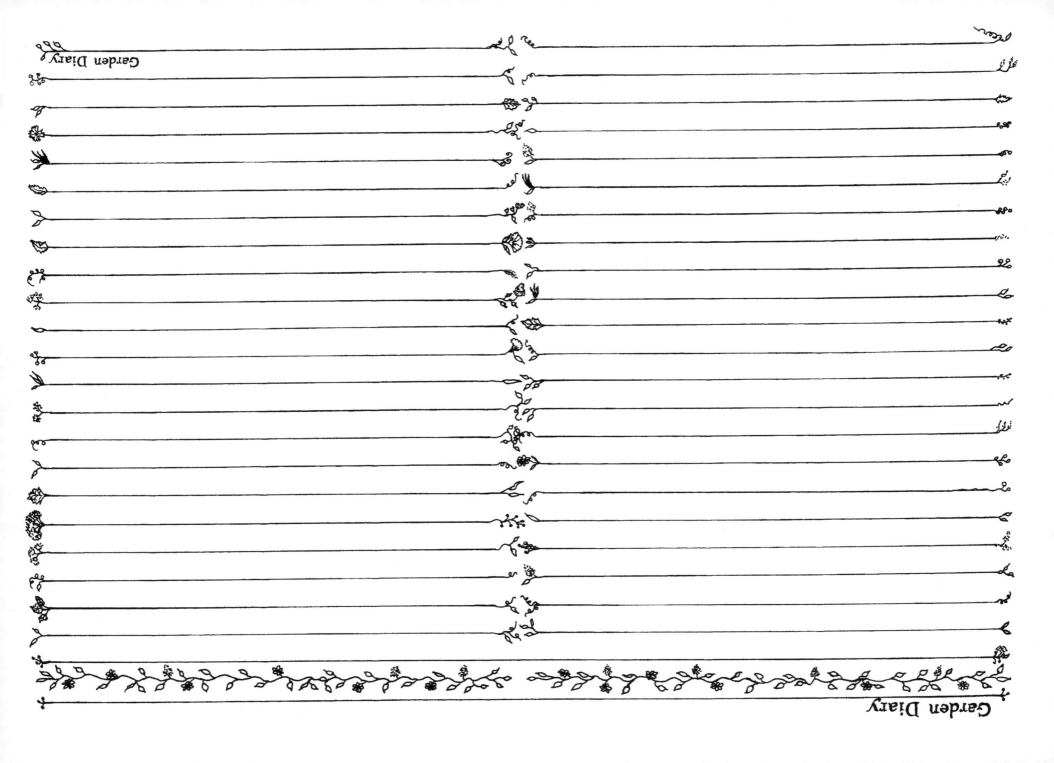

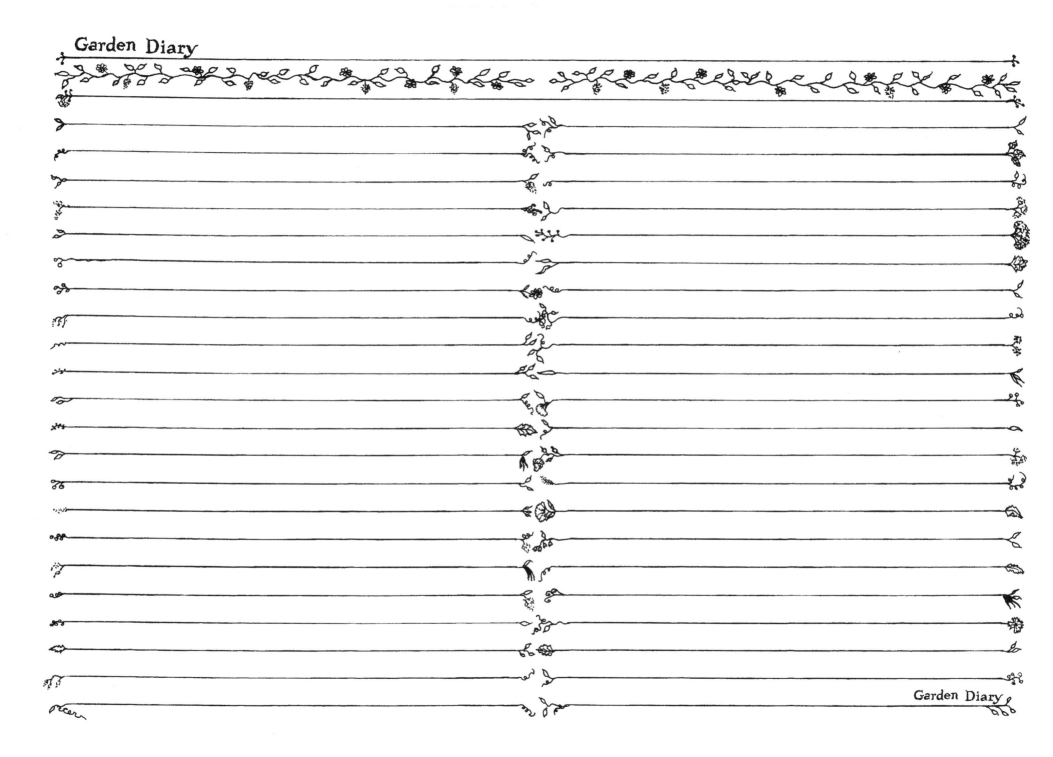

Garden Diary

Garden Diary

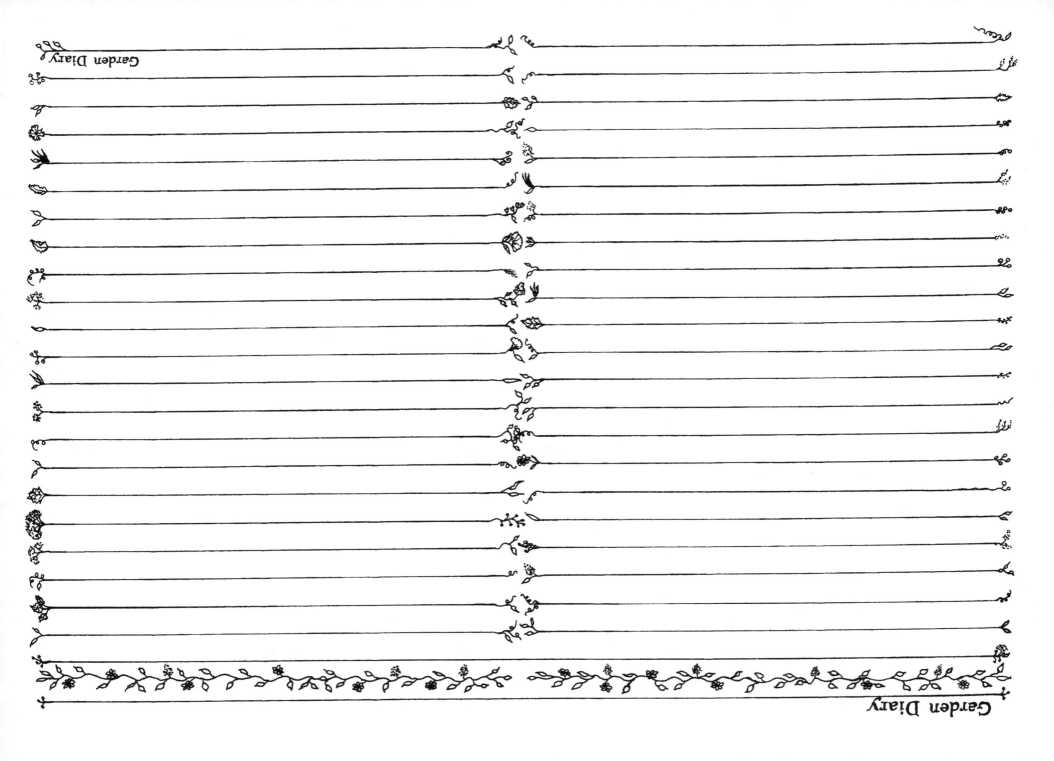

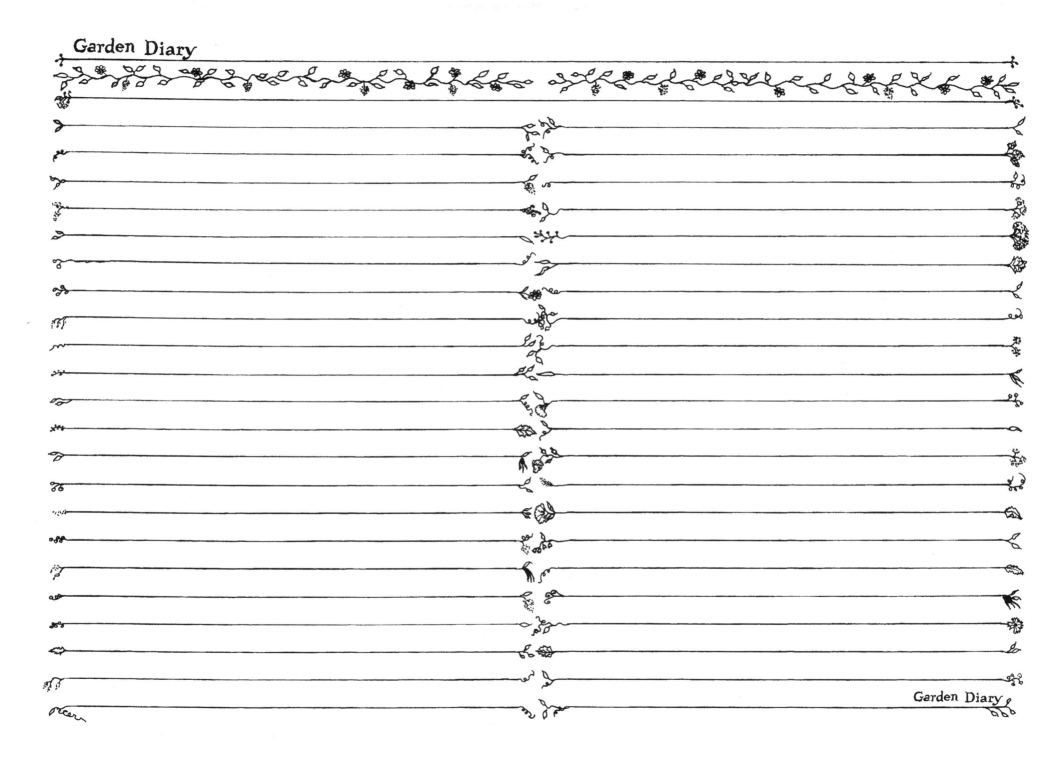

Garden Diary

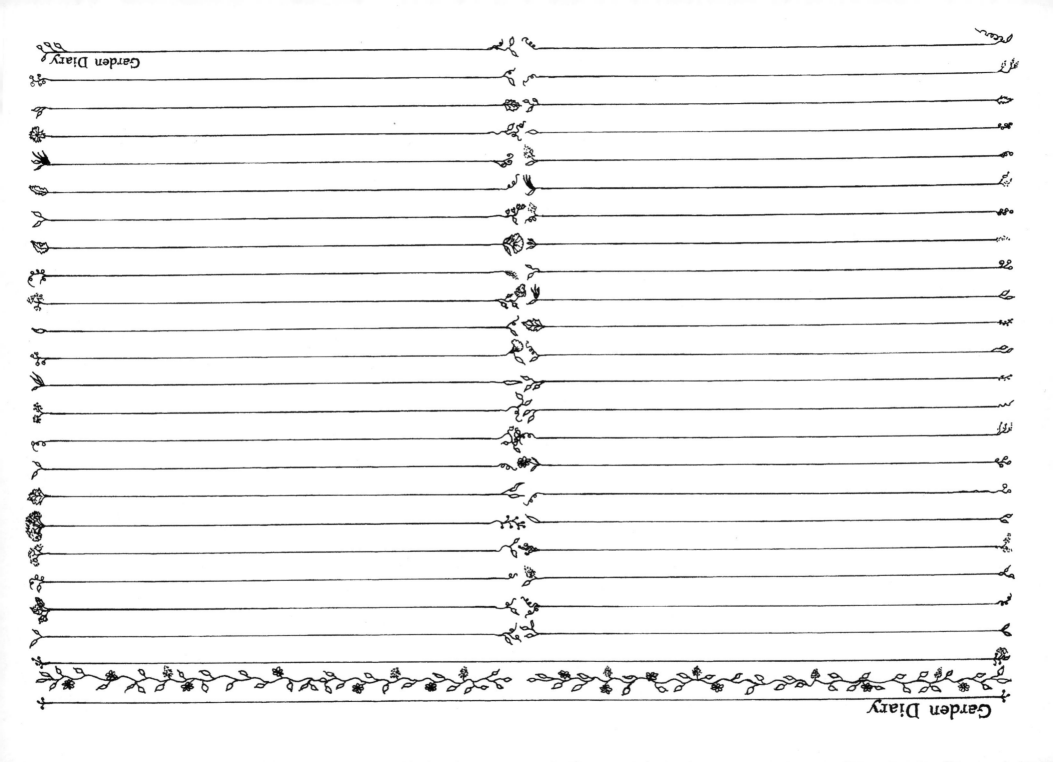

Garden Diary

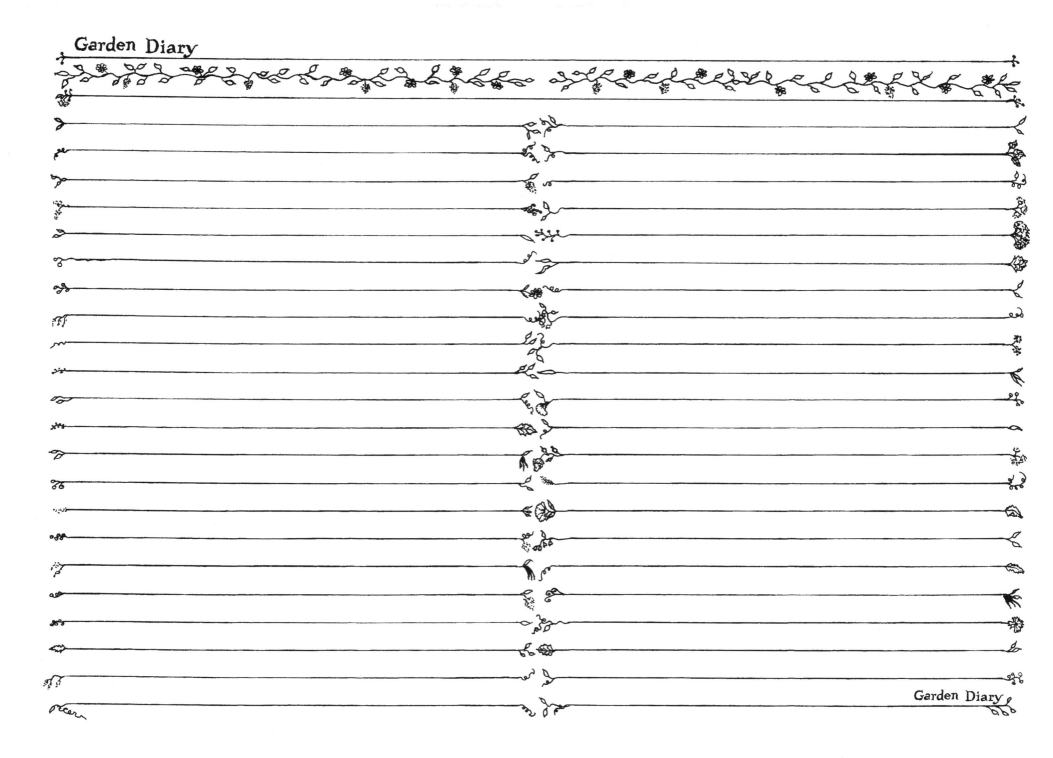

~ Plant Propagation ~

General Guidelines

In general, divide plants when they are not flowering, so that the plant's energy can go to root and leaf growth. Divide spring and summer blooming perennials in fall, and fall bloomers in spring.

If you divide in the spring, allow enough time for roots to settle in before hot weather. Spring division is ideally done in the early spring as soon as the growing tips of the plant have emerged. Spring divided perennials will bloom a little later than usual the first year.

Fall division should take place at least four to six weeks before the ground freezes for the plants to become established.

It's best not to divide perennials on hot, sunny days. Cloudy days are ideal, with several days of light rain in the forecast.

Water plants to be divided thoroughly a day or two before you plan to divide them, so that the ground is soft, but not heavy. Prepare the area that you plan to put your new divisions in before you begin to dig the parent plant.

It's often good to prune the stems and foliage to 6 inches from the ground in order to ease division and to force new growth.

Lift the Parent Plant

Use a sharp pointed spade or spading fork to dig down deep on all four sides of the plant, about 4 to 6 inches away from the plant. Pry underneath with your tool and lift the whole clump to be divided. If the plant is very large and heavy, you may need to cut it into several pieces in place with your shovel before lifting it.

Separate the Plant

Shake or hose off loose soil and remove dead leaves and stems. This will help loosen tangled root balls and make it easier to see what you are doing. Perennials have several different types of root systems. Each of these needs to be treated a bit differently.

Spreading Root Systems

These spreading root systems have matted roots with no distinct pattern. These can crowd out their own centers. Some can be invasive unless divided frequently. They can usually be pulled apart by hand, or cut apart with shears or knife.

Large plants with thickly intertwined roots may need to be separated with digging forks. Put two forks back to back in the center of the plant and use them to pry the pieces apart.

Divide the plants into clumps of three to five vigorous shoots each. Small or weak and woody divisions should be discarded. Discard the center of the clump if it is weaker than the outside edges.

Clumping Root Systems

Clumping root systems originate from a central clump.

It is often necessary to cut through the thick fleshy crowns (the central growing area between the roots and the leaves and stems of the plant) with a heavy, sharp knife. You can also pry apart these roots with back to back digging forks.

Keep at least one developing eye or bud with each division. If larger plants are wanted, keep several eyes.

Rhizome Division

Rhizomes are stems that grow horizontally at or above the soil level. Bearded irises are the most common perennial with this type of root system.

Divide irises any time between a month after flowering until early fall.

Cut and discard the rhizome sections that are one year or older. Also, inspect rhizomes for disease and insect damage. Damaged rhizomes should be trimmed and treated, or discarded if too badly damaged.

Iris divisions should retain a few inches of rhizome and one fan of leaves, trimmed back halfway. Replant with the top of the rhizome just showing above soil level.

Tuberous Roots

Tuberous roots are very similar to rhizomes, but shorter. The tubers should be cut apart with a sharp knife. Every division must have a piece of the original stem and a growth bud attached. After division they can either be replanted or stored for spring planting.

Dividing Large, Tough Roots

If the root mass is very large, or tight and tangled, you can raise the clump 1 to 2 feet off the ground and drop it. This should loosen the root mass, and you can pull the individual plants apart. This is not recommended for plants with brittle roots such as peonies.

Plants that have very tough, vigorous root systems such as ornamental grasses may have to be divided with a shovel, saw or ax. You can also vigorously hose off soil to make the root system easier to work with.

Plant the Divisions

Never allow divisions to dry out. Have plastic bags or pots ready to enclose cuttings as soon as you trim all broken roots and remove anything in surrounding soil that is not part of the plant. Replant divisions at the same depth they were originally. Firm soil around the roots to eliminate air pockets. Water well after planting.

Perennials divided in the fall should be generously mulched the first winter to prevent heaving. The best winter mulch is loose and open, such as pine straw or leaves.

~ Pest and Disease Prevention ~

~ Grow your plants in healthy soil ~

Healthy plants have the best chance of survival against disease and pests. Annual garden cleanup should be performed every fall and into winter. Garden pests and pathogens love to breed and multiply in leftover plant debris, and especially in areas kept moist and warm with matted leaves.

~ Remove and dispose of any . . .
~ diseased, infested or unwanted plants ~

Depending on the disease, either put these in the trash or burn them. Some things, such as poison ivy, and some plant diseases will become airborne if burned. The landfill is the healthier alternative in that case. Healthy plant debris should go into the compost pile or be turned under the soil to decompose.

~ Rotate vegetable crops ~

Many insects and disease-causing organisms overwinter in the soil near their host plants. If you grow the same plant (or a related one) in the same place the next year, you give those pests a head start. Crop rotation can reduce insect damage and minimize exposure to soilborne disease organisms. Wait at least two years before planting the same or related crops, such as onions and garlic, in the same spot. Potatoes, tomatoes, broccoli, cauliflower, brussel sprouts and onions are particularly vulnerable to disease problems when planted in the same location year after year.
Crop rotation also helps keep soil nutrients in balance. A first-year planting of heavy feeders, such as tomatoes and lettuce, can be followed the next year by legumes, which increase the nitrogen in the soil. In the third year, let the soil rest by planting light feeders, such as carrots or beets.

~ Diversify ~

If you place smaller groups of plants throughout the garden, rather than planting all of one plant in one place, it will be less likely that pests or disease will attack the various locations. Interplanting herbs and flowers is another effective way to protect your garden, especially with the use of companion plants. The list of companion plants is too long for inclusion in this book, but can be found online with a simple search.

~ Plant damage that may NOT be from pest and disease ~

~ Wilting ~
~ Is usually due to a lack of moisture. Don't assume plants have enough water if the soil is moist knuckle deep. Make sure the soil is moist to a depth of at least 6" for most vegetable plants and annuals.
~ On the flip side, soil that is too wet can also cause wilting, because the roots are suffocating.
~ Is also a normal response to extreme heat. Wait to see if the plants recover in the evening when temperatures cool. If not, more water or shade may be the answer.
~ Is common for newly transplanted seedlings and other plants that have recently been moved outdoors. Either give them shade or, if still in pots, move them throughout the day to gradually expose them to more time in the sun.

~ Sunburn ~
~ May look like bleached areas on the foliage of new transplants or plants that have been moved from indoors to outdoors. Discoloration will be most pronounced on the leaves most exposed to the sun.

To prevent sunburn, seedlings and other tender plants should be exposed to direct sunlight gradually, over a period of several days. Plants will usually outgrow minor sunburn.

~ Frost Damage ~
~ Will appear as black areas on leaves. The outer leaves will usually show the most damage. Foliage that have been damaged by a late-spring frost will not recover, but the plants will usually recover. Allow damaged leaves to remain until the threat of frost has passed and the plant has begun to show new growth, then remove the affected leaves.

~ Weather Damage ~
Torn foliage can be the result of heavy winds, rain or hail. This makes the plant more vulnerable to invasion by disease. It's usually best to remove damaged foliage. In most cases the leaves will be quickly replaced.

~ Off-Color Foliage ~
~ Is often caused by a nutrient deficiency. Symptom and possible nutrient deficiencies follow:
~ color paler than normal=nitrogen
~ leaf veins are green but the area between them is yellow=iron
~ reddish or purplish cast=phosphorus
~ stunted growth=overall shortage of essential nutrients.

~ Dried Leaf Margins ~
~ May indicate fertilizer burn or wind burn. Always apply fertilizers according to label directions to avoid over-fertilizing. Organic fertilizers rarely cause burning because the nutrients are released slowly over time.

~ Burned Foliage ~
~ especially in one specific area on the plant ~
~ May indicate damage caused by animal urine or herbicide overspray. Spray with water and prune any damaged foliage.

Conversion Charts and Tables

Dry material weight		
1 ounce (avoirdupois)	=	28.4 grams (g)
1 pound (lb)	=	453.6 g
1 kilogram (kg)	=	1,000 g = 2.2 lb
Volume		
1 cubic inch (in^3)	=	16.4 milliliters (ml)
1 cubic foot (ft^3)	=	7.48 gal = 28.3 liters (l)
1 bushel (bu)	=	1.24 ft^3 = 35.2 liters
1 cubic yard (yd^3)	=	21.7 bu = 765 liters
Linear		
1 inch (in)	=	2.54 centimeters (cm)
1 foot (ft)	=	30.48 cm
1 yard (yd)	=	91.44 cm
1 meter (m)	=	100 cm
Area		
1 square inch (in^2)	=	6.45 square centimeters (cm^2)
1 square foot (ft^2)	=	0.09 square meter (m^2)
1 square yard (yd^2)	=	0.84 square meter (m^2)
1 acre (a)	=	0.40 hectare (ha)
1 square mile (M^2)	=	2.59 square kilometer (km^2)

Equivalent quantities of dry materials (wettable powders) for various quantities of water based on recommended pounds per 100 gallons

Water	Recommended Rate					
100 gal	**1 lb**	**2 lb**	**3 lb**	**4 lb**	**5 lb**	**6 lb**
50 gal	½ lb	1 lb	1½ lb	2 lb	2½ lb	3 lb
25 gal	4 oz	8 oz	12 oz	1 lb	1¼ lb	1½ lb
12.5 gal	2 oz	4 oz	6 oz	8 oz	10 oz	¾ lb
5 gal	3 tbs	1½ oz	2½ oz	3¼ oz	4 oz	5 oz
1 gal	1 tsp	2 tsp	1 tbs	4 tsp	5 tsp	2 tbs

***Example*:** The directions specify a rate of 4 lb per 100 gal. water. 1 gal of solution would require 4 tsp of material

Rate of application equivalent table

Rate Per Acre	Rate Per 1000 sq ft	Rate per 100 sq ft
Liquid Materials		
1 pt	¾ tbs	¼ tsp
1 qt	1½ tbs	½ tsp
1 gal	6 tbs	2 tsp
25 gal	$4^2/3$ pt	½ pt
50 gal	$4^2/3$ qt	1 pt
100 gal	$2^1/3$ gal	1 qt
200 gal	$4^2/3$ gal	2 qt
300 gal	7 gal	3 qt
400 gal	9¼ gal	1 gal
500 gal	11½ gal	1¼ gal
Dry Materials		
1 lb	2½ tsp	¼ tsp
3 lb	2¼ tbs	¾ tsp
4 lb	3 tbs	1 tsp
5 lb	4 tbs	1¼ tsp
10 lb	½ cup	2 tsp
100 lb	$2^1/3$ lb	¼ lb
200 lb	$4^2/3$ lb	½ lb
300 lb	7 lb	¾ lb
400 lb	9¼ lb	1 lb
500 lb	11½ lb	1¼ lb

Dilution of liquid pesticides at various concentrations

Dilution	Amount Desired			
	1 Gal	**3 Gal**	**5 Gal**	**15 Gal**
1-100	2 tbs + 2 tsp	½ cup	¾ cup + 5 tsp	1 cup + 3 tbs
1-200	4 tsp	¼ cup	6½ tbs	½ cup + 2 tbs
1-400	2 tsp	2 tbs	3 tbs	4 tbs + 2½ tsp
1-800	1 tsp	1 tbs	1 tbs + 2 tsp	3 tbs + 2½ tsp
1-1000	¾ tsp	2¼ tsp	1 tbs + 1 tsp	1 pt + ½ cup

Coverage estimates for perlite, peat, topsoil and straw

Thickness	4 cu ft	6 cu ft	1 cu yd*	1 Bale	
	Perlite	Canadian peat (compressed)	Peat mulches		
			Topsoil, etc.	Pinestraw	Wheatstraw
2 in	28 sq ft	72 sq ft	162 sq ft	90 sq ft	180 sq ft
1 in	48 sq ft	144 sq ft	324 sq ft	180 sq ft	360 sq ft
½ in	96 sq ft	288 sq ft	648 sq ft	360 sq ft	720 sq ft
¼ in	192 sq ft	576 sq ft	1296 sq ft	720 sq ft	1440 sq ft

Liquid Measurement Conversion Table

Units of Measure:

Gallons (gal)	Quarts (qt)	Pints (pt)	Fluid Ounces (fl oz)	Cups (C)	Tablespoons (tbs)	Teaspoons (tsp)	Milliliters (ml)	Cubic Centimeters (cc)	Liters (l)
1	4	8	128	16					
	1	2	32	4					
		1	16	2	32				
			1	1/8	2	6	30		
				1	16	48	240		
					1	3	15		
						1	5		
							1	1	
							1000	1000	1

Conversion Charts and Tables

About the Author

Joy comes from a long line of farmers, but it wasn't until she worked for J. Franklin Styer Nurseries, a major contributor to the Philadelphia Flower Show, that she learned that not everything should be planted in rows. She and her father still laugh about his single line of tulips across the front yard. After his own stint working for a nursery he has developed his property into a miniature Longwood Gardens.

The Garden Journal, Record and Log book is the result of knowledge gained from her father, the library and co-workers at Styer Nurseries, her experience running the Lifewerks Giving Garden ~ a food pantry garden ~ as well as maintenance of gardens at three properties.